COLONEL
BLOOD

COLONEL BLOOD

The Man who STOLE the CROWN JEWELS

DAVID C. HANRAHAN

SUTTON PUBLISHING

This book was first published in 2003 by
Sutton Publishing Limited · Phoenix Mill
Thrupp · Stroud · Gloucestershire · GL5 2BU

This paperback edition first published in 2004

British Library Cataloguing in Publication Data
A catalogue record for this book is available from the British Library.

ISBN 0 7509 3328 3

Typeset in 11/12.5 pt Photina.
Typesetting and origination by
Sutton Publishing Limited.
Printed and bound in Great Britain by
J.H. Haynes & Co. Ltd, Sparkford.

CONTENTS

PREFACE AND ACKNOWLEDGEMENTS

Colonel Thomas Blood, the man who stole the Crown Jewels, was the most notorious outlaw of his day. His character mixed defiance, pride and courage with a desire for risk-taking and notoriety. The times in which he lived were themselves momentous, with events such as the Civil War, the usurpation and execution of a monarch, the rule of Oliver Cromwell and ultimately the restoration of the monarchy. The course of Blood's own life is inextricably bound up not only with these events but also with the lives of a number of other wonderfully colourful characters such as James Butler, the 1st Duke of Ormonde, Charles II and George Villiers, the 2nd Duke of Buckingham. All of these people play fascinating roles in the life of Thomas Blood. This book examines the lives and influences of these characters as well as their particular and often bizarre connection with Blood himself. The story of his life and times is a colourful one, full of treachery, courage, intrigue, ambition, roguery and religious fanaticism.

I wish to thank the following bodies and their staff in particular: the Hardiman Library, National University of Ireland, Galway; the National Library of Ireland; the British Library; the Public Record Office, London; the Bodleian Library, Oxford; the National Portrait Gallery, London; HM Tower of London; the Royal Armouries Museum, Leeds; the Local Studies Library, Ennis. Sincere thanks are due to Chris Gravett (Senior Curator, Tower History) and Bridget Clifford (Senior Curator, Library), both with the Royal Armouries at HM Tower of London. Chris kindly facilitated my visit and Bridget allowed me to see Colonel Blood's dagger and found every relevant document in the library. A word of thanks to Yeoman Serjeant Phil Wilson, who whisked me into the Chapel Royal of St Peter ad Vincula between guided tours so that I could see Talbot Edward's tombstone.

I also want to take this opportunity to express my gratitude to the following: the Academic Planning and Resource Committee and the Faculty of Arts at NUI, Galway, for awarding me a PhD Fellowship; the staff of the Education Department, NUI, Galway, for their kindness to me both as postgraduate student and lecturer; Tuamgraney National School from where I have been on career-break these past few years; and Mary Immaculate College of Education, Limerick, where my odyssey into third-level education began.

My thanks to all at Sutton Publishing, especially Christopher Feeney who saw merit in this project from the beginning, Matthew Brown and Jane Entrican for their editorial care and attention. I am grateful to my agent, David O'Leary, for sharing my enthusiasm about Colonel Blood. Finally, a special word of thanks must go to my family, my brothers and their families, in particular my parents, my wonderful children Aisling and Michael, and my wife Margaret without whom, quite simply, none of this would have been possible.

PROLOGUE

In May 1671 four armed men headed by Colonel Thomas Blood walked into the Tower of London and stole some of the Crown Jewels. With the Keeper of the Jewel House left for dead, the gang made off with the crown and the orb, leaving the partly filed sceptre behind on the floor. The *London Gazette* for 8–11 May 1671 carried the following account of what was surely one of the most remarkable crimes of the century:

> Whitehall, May 9. This morning about seven of the clock, four men coming to Mr. Edwards, Keeper of the Jewel House in the Tower, desired to see the Regal Crown remaining in his custody, he carries them into the room where they were kept, and shows them; but according to the villainous design they it seems came upon, immediately they clap a gag of a strange form into the old man's mouth; who making what noise and resistance he could, they stabbed him a deep wound in the belly with a stiletto, adding several other dangerous wounds on the head with a small beetle they had with them, as is believed, to beat together and flatten the Crown, to make it the more easily portable; which having, together with the Ball, put into Bags, they had to that purpose brought with them; they fairly walked out, leaving the old man grovelling on the ground, gagged and pinioned . . .[1]

To contemporary readers this account of the daring robbery must have seemed incredible. Who would have the audacity to walk in and remove such precious items from a place as secure as the Tower of London? A deed like this had never been attempted before. These were audacious thieves who surely intended to be noticed. However, readers would have been less surprised at the boldness of the enterprise as they read on and it became clear that the leader of this gang was 'that notorious traytor and incendiary', Thomas Blood.[2]

Blood, a Protestant rebel with a rough face, a large nose and an oversized thumb, had long been the scourge of the kingdom. Since he had successfully managed to evade arrest for many years and had been involved in a number of daring enterprises, it would have appeared quite possible that he might attempt this defiant act of stealing the King's own crown from the Tower.

1

TROUBLED TIMES

Thomas Blood, a man who has been described as 'the most famous and successful of English law breakers', was no ordinary criminal.[1] He was born into the Protestant land-owning class in Ireland and it was only through the vicissitudes of circumstance that he eventually found himself on the wrong side of the law, leading a life of rebellion, gaol-breaking, kidnap and robbery. His grandfather, Edmund Blood, was a member of an English Presbyterian family from Mackney House (now Makeney), Duffield, Derbyshire, who came to Ireland in 1595. Unlike most of his co-religionists Captain Edmund Blood chose not to go to Ulster but went instead to the picturesque county of Clare, west of the River Shannon. He arrived there with his small group of cavalry-men to serve as an officer under Lord Inchiquin in the so-called Nine Years' War that was raging between the English settlers and the native Irish.

The early years of the seventeenth century in Ireland were ones in which a state-sponsored Anglicisation of the country was under way. Settlers were being encouraged to move to Ireland with the incentive of financial support. This meant that Edmund Blood found his feet pretty quickly in his new country. The Bloods settled first at Kilnaboy Castle and later Bohersallagh House, with two hundred acres of land, near Corofin.[2] Captain Blood also controlled a small harbour in the north of County Clare, from where he plied the lucrative trade of demanding tolls from passing shipping vessels going to the busy port of Galway. His demands were backed up by a number of boats with well-armed crews.[3]

In 1613 Ennis, the capital town of County Clare, received a royal charter as a borough. Edmund was one of the twelve men, all Protestants, who were named as free burgesses of the town. These were the people who had the honour of voting for the two Members of Parliament who would represent the town in Dublin. In fact Edmund was himself elected as one of those MPs for Ennis, serving from 1613 to 1615.

On their way to Ireland Edmund's unfortunate wife gave birth to their first child on board ship somewhere in the middle of the Irish Sea. Luckily, both mother and child survived the experience and the child, a boy, was aptly named Neptune after the Roman god of the sea! Edmund and his wife went on to have three other sons, Edmund, Thomas and William. Neptune later became the Very Reverend Blood DD, Dean of Kilfernora Cathedral in County Clare, a position he held for thirty years. He fought for the King at Oxford,[4] married three times, lived to nearly a hundred and was succeeded as Dean by his son of the same name.[5] Neptune chose to continue Edmund's morally and legally suspect practice of demanding tolls from passing ships. These tolls only came to an end with the rule of Cromwell, who would allow no such private enterprise. Although the Cromwellians burned his boats and dispersed his men, they did give Dr Blood three grants of confiscated land in compensation for the loss of business.[6]

Meanwhile Edmund Blood's second son, Thomas, settled in the townland of Sarney in County Meath, not far from Dublin, where he made his living as a blacksmith and ironworker. It seems he managed to build up quite a substantial business for himself, operating out of ports in both Ireland and England.[7] In around 1618 his wife had given birth to a baby boy whom they christened Thomas after his father, and who grew up to become the infamous Thomas Blood of this story.[8] Of him it was said that 'His birth was such as gave him those advantages that usually distinguish a man from the Vulgar' and the education he received was 'strict and sober'.[9]

When Blood was about seven, James I died and was succeeded as King of England, Scotland and Ireland by his son, Charles I. It was well known that the new King was small in stature, aloof, and had a stammer. In fact he would not have become King at all had his elder brother, Henry, not died when Charles was still a child.

The new King's marriage to the French Roman Catholic Princess Henrietta-Maria greatly perturbed not only his Protestant subjects but also his Parliament. It was a Parliament with which he soon began to come into serious conflict. A major cause of discontent among MPs was Charles's religious policy of supporting the High Church style of Anglicanism associated with William Laud, the Archbishop of Canterbury.[10] The beliefs and ritual being rigorously promoted by Laud were seen by many, especially those known as the Puritans, as too close to Roman Catholicism. Chief among these practices were the compulsory use of the 1559 Prayer Book, the elevated status of bishops and parish clergy, and the belief that the only way to God was through priests and sacraments. In addition, Puritans were scandalised by the renovation of church buildings in which stained glass was encouraged, and by the presence of statues and railed-off altars. To make matters more tense, Archbishop Laud was a man not shy of using persecution in the pursuit of his aims, including, frequently, the removal of ears!

The Puritans, who had a strong voice in Parliament, became dominant among those who objected to these policies. They wanted to 'purify' the Church of England of all Roman Catholic influences and consequently loathed the

1559 Prayer Book. They wanted bishops abolished, and were opposed to the celebration of 'popish' feasts such as Easter and Christmas. For them 'the word of God' alone counted.

Charles I was also a strong believer in what was known as the Royal Prerogative or the divine right of the King to rule. The Prerogative referred to those special powers possessed by the King in his role as monarch, described by constitutional lawyer Sir William Blackstone as 'that special pre-eminence the King hath over and above all persons and out of the common law in right of his regal dignity'.[11] Among the privileges enshrined in the Prerogative were that the King alone had the right to determine foreign policy and that only he could prorogue or dissolve Parliament. A prorogation of Parliament meant that it could be called together again without an election, whereas dissolution necessitated the calling of one. Charles's authoritarian attitude towards ruling and his dislike of being challenged by Parliament on any of his powers only exacerbated a deteriorating political situation.

Blood was only around ten in 1628 when in these tense circumstances Charles's insistence that Parliament come up with the money to pay for his military expenses through taxation developed into a burning issue. The MPs presented Charles with a document known as the Petition of Right by means of which Parliament intended to alter the Royal Prerogative in exchange for the war expenses sought by the King. At first Charles, forced by circumstances, accepted the Petition but in 1629, after a number of acrimonious exchanges, decided instead to dispense with Parliament and have several of its leaders thrown into gaol. He then went on to govern without a Parliament for the next eleven years.

In 1637, when Charles, in line with Archbishop Laud's teachings, decided to impose changes to the Anglican liturgy and Prayer Book in Scotland, it led to rioting among the Presbyterians there. The revolt grew and Charles urgently needed funds to put together a military response.

The Scottish Presbyterians, thereafter known as the Covenanters, signed the National Covenant in 1638 in which they pledged to preserve their form of worship and church government in Scotland. In order to raise funds for war, Charles was forced to call a Parliament for the first time in eleven years. This so-called Short Parliament sat for just one month in 1640. However, the MPs began to make demands in return for raising the necessary money, drawing up a list of public grievances and demanding that Charles make peace with the Covenanters. Charles, infuriated by this, would not agree and attacked the Scots anyway.

The war did not go well for the King, and the Scots managed to cross the border and take Newcastle and Durham. Added to this major embarrassment, the King's financial situation was growing ever more precarious and later in 1640 he found himself in the unenviable position of having to call yet another Parliament. This time the so-called Long Parliament led by John Pym was not to be so easily dispensed with. It impeached Archbishop Laud and another of the King's chief advisers, Sir Thomas Wentworth, the 1st Earl of Strafford, and had them both thrown into the Tower of London. The King had no option but to accept Parliament's demands for reforms, including more religious liberties for the Scots and the concession that in future Parliament could not be dissolved without its own consent.

In addition to all this, when Blood was in his early twenties tensions were very high in the country of his birth. In 1641 those tensions, caused by Roman Catholic discontent, boiled over into a violent rebellion in Ireland. The Roman Catholics had for a long time been unhappy at their loss of land to the Protestant settlers who had been planted, mainly in Ulster, by the King's father, James I. These 'adventurers' from Scotland and England had been allowed to take over four million acres of good land while the native Roman Catholic Irish were forced to survive on much poorer holdings.[12] The Roman Catholics also objected to the suppression of their religion, which was the majority one. They also feared greatly the type of repressive religious legislation that a Parliament so heavily influenced by Puritans might introduce in Ireland. The population of Ireland at the time consisted of a religious mix that included native Irish Roman Catholics, many 'old English' settlers (both Roman Catholics and Protestants) and the Presbyterians who had arrived as part of the 'Ulster Plantation'. Although the Roman Catholic 'old English' had no love for the native Irish, they did share their religious concerns.

In response to this outbreak of hostilities in Ireland, Charles once again had to turn to Parliament in order to raise the funds necessary to mount a military response. However, mainly because of the fear that any such army might be used against themselves, the MPs refused. Furthermore, they issued a document entitled the 'Grand Remonstrance on the State of the Kingdom', which was heavily influenced by Pym, in which they ascribed all the present difficulties to what they termed 'the oppressions of the Popish party'.[13] Among other things the document demanded that all bishops be dismissed from Parliament and the King's Council, that all Crown land in Ireland be preserved, and that from then on Parliament should control the King's choice of ministers. After the Christmas recess Charles responded by going to Westminster Hall with an armed force to arrest Pym and four others. However, these leading figures knew that he was coming and made sure not to be there. By 1642 the scene was set for what is now known as the English Civil War. It was a war that would divide Charles's subjects down the middle and bring his life, as well as his reign, to an end. It has been described as a war 'more the consequence of pilot error than mechanical failure'.[14]

It was this war that brought to prominence a man who was to play such a significant part in future events in the British Isles. The war enabled Oliver Cromwell, a brilliant military strategist, to utilise his skills. A committed Puritan and hater of Roman Catholics, he became leader of the Roundhead army. Ten years earlier Cromwell had first become a Member of Parliament for Huntingdon. When he was nearly forty he experienced a deeply religious 'rebirth' to the ideals and beliefs of Puritanism. It was a conviction he held devoutly for the rest of his life. In 1636 he received a substantial inheritance of land and property in the city of Ely and was elected Member of Parliament for Cambridge in 1641.

At the outbreak of the Civil War Cromwell returned home to Huntingdon, where he raised a volunteer force of about a hundred men to challenge what he perceived as the Catholic-friendly King Charles I.[15] By 1643 his troop of horse numbered 2,000 and had earned for themselves the name 'Ironsides', mainly as a result of their leader's reputation in battle. With each engagement in the war Cromwell's fame grew and his proficiency in the tactics of war assured his rapid rise through the military ranks.

The military might of Parliament was greatly boosted by their signing of the Solemn League and Covenant with the Presbyterian Covenanters in Scotland in 1643. In return for the dismissal of all bishops and the Church of England becoming Presbyterian, the Covenanters agreed to support the English Parliament.

The first Civil War came to an end in 1646, when Charles I was forced to surrender. He chose not to give himself up to the Parliamentary side, but instead went to the Scots, hoping to receive better treatment from them. They attempted to get him to convert, while his wife urged him from the continent to agree to the establishment of an official Presbyterian Church, which she believed would provide him with a Scots army.[16] However, all negotiations failed and the Scots handed him over to the English Parliament in 1647. Hostilities did not end there. A second Civil War followed in 1648, when the King managed to escape custody and ally himself with the Scots. But once again Cromwell's leadership and military abilities brought him decisive victory.

Cromwell then went on to suppress all remaining Royalist support to become the most powerful person in England. Parliamentarians who refused to pass an Act of Treason forbidding any further negotiations with the King were ejected, and the remainder, the so-called Rump Parliament, proceeded to have the King tried. The result of this was that Charles I was beheaded in London on 30 January 1649. The monarchy and the House of Lords were abolished, England was declared a Commonwealth and Oliver Cromwell became Chairman of the Council of State and in effect ruler.

Meanwhile, bloody rebellion had been raging in Ireland since 1641. Thomas Blood was a young man of around twenty-three at the outbreak of hostilities there. His family had done well under the Stuart monarchy in Ireland. According to a civil survey, his father had owned 220 acres of land in the townland of Sarney in Dunboyne, County Meath, since at least 1640.[17] The records also show that an Edmond Blood, probably his grandfather, owned 70 acres of land and property, which included a mill, in the town of Dunboyne at the same time. Coming from such a family, it is not surprising that at the early age of twenty-one Blood himself was appointed a Justice of the Peace.

Since both he and his father were committed Protestants, it is little wonder that with the outbreak of the Roman Catholic rebellion in Ireland Blood began his military career by fighting on the Royalist side against the Catholics.[18] He may have been a captain in the army of Charles I under Sir Lewis Dyve,[19] and it was also claimed that he had served under Monck in Ireland.[20] Prince Rupert later said that he remembered him as 'a very stout, bold fellow in the royal service'.[21] His efforts in the royal service probably account for the fact that in 1643 Charles granted him the towns and lands of Sarney, Braystown and Foylestown in the barony of Dunboyne, County Meath and 500 acres of 'unprofitable mountain' in Glenmalure, County Wicklow.[22]

In October 1641 the leader of the Catholic rebels, Sir Phelim O'Neill, had issued a proclamation in which he declared the defence of Irish liberty, demanded an end to Protestant plantations and all religious repression, but also affirmed his allegiance to King Charles I. Ironically, the rebels claimed to be defending not only their own rights but also the King's against this rogue Puritan Parliament. The accomplished military leader, Eoghan Ruadh O'Neill, took over as Supreme Commander of the Irish Forces in 1642 and by the end of that year had most of the country under his control. Protestant planters were seen as legitimate targets by the Roman Catholics who believed the planters would be used to implement any repressive religious legislation introduced by the Puritan Parliament. Consequently many were attacked and brutally slaughtered. By 1642 most were forced to flee to the few remaining uncaptured fortresses for protection.

In County Clare, Blood's uncle, the Revd Neptune Blood, although not killed, was a victim of intimidation according to a statement made by him before Commissioners appointed to take evidence upon oath in 1642. He was, according to his testimony, 'despoiled of goods worth £180, as well as of church livings worth £140 yearly. . . . His house at Killinaboy was pulled down . . . his cattle were taken away'.[23]

The Commander-in-Chief of the King's army, James Butler, 12th Earl of Ormonde, did his best to stem this tide of Roman Catholic aggression but the English force in Ireland was badly provided for in terms of essentials such as food and clothing. Although the Scottish Parliament sent General Monroe with 10,000 much better provisioned men to crush the rebellion, the rebels continued to enjoy the upper hand.

The Confederate Catholics of Ireland, as the rebels now called themselves, set up headquarters in Kilkenny. They included both native Irish and 'old English' Roman

Catholics, although the alliance between them never really overcame their long-held mutual distrust and enmity. However, as they watched events unfolding in the Civil War in England they became ever more concerned. They agreed that the Crown was a far better choice for them than an anti-Catholic, Puritan Parliament. Ironically for an Irish rebel group, their motto became 'Pro Deo, Pro Rege, Pro Hibernia unanimis' – 'United for God, King and Ireland'.[24]

His difficulties at home made the King anxious that a cessation be brought to the fighting in Ireland. Therefore the Duke of Ormonde found himself in the position of having to negotiate a treaty with his Roman Catholic enemies. It was no easy task for the staunchly Protestant Ormonde. Negotiations got under way and eventually a one-year cessation was agreed to in September 1643 and extended several times until it eventually led to the peace treaty of March 1646. However, real peace on the ground was difficult to achieve. O'Neill in Ulster refused to accept the treaty and duly ignored it. The Pope's representative, the Papal Nuncio Rinuccini, who had arrived in Ireland, denounced it. Monroe also refused to accept the treaty as he was now following orders from Parliament. The fighting continued and to add to the general mayhem Lord Inchiquin in Munster defected from the Royalist side to the Parliamentarian and began killing Roman Catholics.[25]

An alliance such as that brokered between the Royalist army under Ormonde and the Confederate Catholics was unpalatable to many devoted Protestants. It was probably this event that caused Blood and his father to switch their allegiance from King to Parliament. Father and son went to England to fight with the Parliamentary forces there. The father is said by one writer to have 'spent his fortune on the cause' and he died during this period.[26] The son fought first under Fairfax and later under Cromwell himself. He was promoted to the rank of Lieutenant in Cromwell's army, which seems to have been the only genuine military rank he ever held, despite the fact that throughout his life he promoted himself regularly!

In July of 1647, with the rebel army quickly approaching Dublin, Ormonde, who had never been happy about his alliance with the Roman Catholics, decided to surrender it and the other towns under his control to the Parliamentary troops. He had, it seems, received a message from the King telling him that if he had to give up his garrison he should give it to the English rather than the Irish.[27] After a stay in England Ormonde fled to join the King's son, the young Prince Charles, on the continent.

In September 1648 the Irish called for the Prince's help following a number of damaging defeats against the Parliamentary forces, and Ormonde was sent back to Ireland once again as the King's Lord Lieutenant. In January 1649 another peace treaty was signed under which free exercise of the Roman Catholic religion in Ireland was granted and the Supreme Council of the Confederates duly appointed Ormonde as commander of all the anti-Parliament troops in Ireland. He went on to lead the fight in Ireland against the Parliamentarians with considerable success until the arrival of Cromwell.

Once the Civil War was over and he was in control of England, Cromwell's next task was to assert his leadership over this volatile situation in Ireland. In August 1649, with the titles of Commander-in-Chief of the Irish Expeditionary Force and Lord Lieutenant of Ireland, he sailed to Ireland accompanied by over twelve thousand men to begin his subjugation of the country. Blood was among those men travelling back to his native country.[28]

The scene was set for a bloody struggle. With the arrival of Cromwell, Eoghan Ruadh O'Neill decided that his best option was to join forces with Ormonde against the common enemy, pledging his allegiance to the King as he did so. However, O'Neill's death in November 1649 was to prevent the renowned Irish militarist from taking on the Cromwellian army in battle.

Before long, Cromwell's considerable military abilities and superior artillery power began to gain the upper hand in Ireland. His most infamous victories of the campaign were achieved at Drogheda and Wexford, and soon the subjugation of Ireland had been accomplished.

It was now time for those who had contributed to the successful Parliamentary campaign in Ireland to be rewarded and those who had opposed the regime to be punished. In March 1642, in order to crush the Irish rebellion, Parliament had passed the Adventurers' Act, which promised to set aside land in Ireland for those who were willing to advance money for the cause, known as 'adventurers'. The idea was to throw the cost of suppressing the rebellion back on the Irish themselves. In fact, Oliver Cromwell himself was one of those adventurers who had put money forward. As it happened, much of the money raised had been spent on Parliament's fight against the King. None the less, the confiscation of land was now put into effect by means of the Cromwellian Act of Settlement (1652) and the Act of Satisfaction (1653).

Ten Irish counties, including Waterford, Limerick, Tipperary, Queen's County and Meath, were nominated for the satisfaction of the claims of those who had supported the cause, namely the adventurers and soldiers.[29] Among the estates to be confiscated in their entirety were those belonging to people who had taken part in the Irish rebellion prior to the establishment of the Confederate government at Kilkenny, all Roman Catholic priests who had been involved in the rebellion and a number of prominent people mentioned by name, including the Duke of Ormonde. In order to free enough land to reward the adventurers and soldiers, other landowners, who had never taken part in the rebellion, were also to lose a proportion of their estates and be relocated west of the River Shannon to the province of Connacht or the county of Clare, where they would receive land. As one writer puts it, many a land-holder was 'forced to exchange his fertile patrimony in Meath or Tipperary for a barren bog or rocky mountainside in Connaught or Clare'.[30] The Cromwellian confiscation of land in Ireland not only subjected thousands of people to tremendous suffering, but the effects on land ownership in Ireland were to be significant and long-lasting.

Blood, as one of those who had fought as a Cromwellian soldier, was now duly rewarded for his services with a grant of confiscated Irish lands and by being made a Justice of the Peace.

In England Cromwell dismissed the Rump Parliament in 1653 by bringing his soldiers to the House of Commons and in its place appointed the so-called Barebones Parliament, which lasted only a few months. Finally, and it seems reluctantly, Oliver Cromwell took over the ruling of the state himself as 'Lord Protector of England, Ireland and Scotland' with a Parliament of one house and a Council of twenty-one advisers. The Cromwellian age had begun.

2

LOVE IN LANCASHIRE

It was during the Civil War that the young Lieutenant Blood had marched into Lancashire with the Parliamentary army to take part in the struggle in the north. While there, he had become acquainted with another young man fighting alongside him called Thomas Holcroft. Holcroft's family owned Holcroft Hall in the nearby village of Culcheth, not far from Winwick and Warrington and at that time in the county of Lancashire.

The Holcrofts could claim a long and illustrious history in their small community. In the thirteenth century Gilbert de Culcheth – who had four daughters and no sons – owned a significant estate in the area. He divided his estate up between his daughters – one daughter took the estate and name of Pesfurlong when she married, and another that of Risley. The two other daughters married a pair of brothers, Richard and Thomas de Hindley, with one taking the name Culcheth while the other took that of Holcroft. It is from these Holcrofts that the family living there in the 1600s was descended.[1]

When Blood was introduced to the family by his friend, its head was Colonel John Holcroft, a committed Parliamentarian who had been MP for Liverpool in the Short Parliament from 13 April to 5 May 1640. He had become Mayor of Liverpool in 1644 and MP for Wigan until 1648, when Pride's Purge led to his ejection.

In addition to his son Thomas, Colonel Holcroft had another son, Charles, and three daughters, Maria, Isabella and Rachel. According to one writer the portrait of Colonel Holcroft's eldest daughter Maria does not show her to be a very pretty woman, but from her actions we can see that she was a very determined one.[2] It seems that the Colonel had decided that she should marry a local gentleman, but that was before Maria had met the courageous Lieutenant Thomas Blood.

We can only imagine what happened at that first meeting when Thomas Holcroft introduced his sister to his friend. We do know that there must have been a strong and immediate attraction between them, for although Blood left Holcroft Hall shortly afterwards to fight with Cromwell in Ireland, he and Maria did not forget each other.

Once Ireland was under Cromwellian control, Blood returned to England to continue the wooing of Maria Holcroft. But their relationship was not welcomed. Maria's father objected strongly to it and refused to give them his blessing. However, Maria was obviously a strong character and the romance continued undeterred until on 21 June 1650 at Newchurch, Culcheth, Thomas Blood and Maria Holcroft were married by the local curate, William Leigh. The entry in the Newchurch parish register reads: 'Thomas Bloud gens et Maria Holcroft matrimonio copulati vicessimo primo die Junni anno Domi, 1650'.[3]

Sadly for the newlyweds the troubled times in which they lived meant that Blood had business to attend to in Ireland, and soon after their wedding he left. As it happened, Maria would not see him again for two years. While he was away he missed the birth of their first child, a son named Thomas after his father and grandfather. The child's baptism is recorded in the church register as 'Thomas filius Thome Blood ari. Baptizatus 30mo Martii anno Domi, 1651'.[4]

Maria met her husband once again on 31 August 1652 at the wedding of her close friend, Eleanor Birch, and her brother, Thomas Holcroft. Maria must have been pleased to have her husband and young son united under the same roof. Perhaps she decided that her husband would not leave without them again, and this time when Blood returned to Ireland both she and the baby accompanied him. Conditions were much more favourable now for her to accompany him to the country of his birth. Blood had acquired an estate under the Cromwellian land settlement as a reward for his services in the war, and Henry Cromwell had appointed him a Commissioner of Parliament in Ireland. In addition he was entrusted with the duty of hunting down and capturing those Roman Catholic rebels known as Tories who were creating a lot of difficulties for the authorities at the time.

For Maria circumstances must have seemed settled in her new home, where she could now raise her family and live contentedly. However, although she did not know it yet, the family of Thomas Blood would never lead such an ordinary life.

3

A MAN OF RELIGION

All was going well for Blood and his young family in Ireland until the night in September 1658 when, in the midst of a raging storm, Oliver Cromwell died of natural causes at the age of fifty-nine. It was controversially claimed that as he lay dying Cromwell had unexpectedly nominated his son Richard as the new Lord Protector in place of his more able son, Henry. Richard Cromwell inherited a difficult situation. A very expensive war against the Dutch had put the country in debt to such an extent that incoming revenues were insufficient to cope. Palpable unease was beginning to grow in many quarters, especially among the army, where arrears of pay were mounting. Richard also annoyed many army officers by taking personal control of the army instead of appointing an experienced officer as they wanted.

It was decided to call a Parliament to help solve these problems. However, the revelation to the MPs of the dire financial situation of the state only added to the confusion and uncertainty. Senior army officers, now known as the Council of Officers, demanded that Parliament be dissolved when it declared that they should not meet without Richard's prior approval. At first Richard attempted to dismiss the Council but then had to make a U-turn and dismiss Parliament instead.

The Council of Officers was now in control and decided to recall the Rump Parliament. Richard Cromwell's term of rule effectively came to an end when the Rump dismissed him. He later abdicated and went into exile, having been in power for only eight months. However, mutual distrust between the Council of Officers and the Rump Parliament meant that they could achieve nothing, and after only a few months a dispute led to the occupation of the House of Commons by Major General John Lambert. The Rump was ousted from power.

It was in these circumstances that Henry Cromwell also vacated his post as Lord Lieutenant of Ireland and a political vacuum was created that allowed a number of Protestants to capture Dublin Castle and place Colonel Jones, who was Ludlow's deputy there, under arrest. Blood was one of those involved in this action, which mirrored what Lambert had done in London.[1]

General George Monck, commander of the English army in Scotland, condemned Lambert's actions in London and decided that it was in the best interest of the country for him to march south and take control himself. Monck defeated Lambert's army and restored the Rump once again. He also ordered the group in Dublin, of which Blood was a member, to release Colonel Jones. They complied. In 1660 Monck forced the Rump to dissolve itself and a new Parliament was elected.

Meanwhile, prompt negotiations were held with the deceased King's son, Charles, which led to an agreement known as the Declaration of Breda by which the Republic came to an end and the monarchy was restored to power in the person of King Charles II. Among the proposals of the Declaration were the promise of an amnesty and 'a liberty to tender consciences', which meant that those of differing religious beliefs, such as Roman Catholics and non-Anglican Protestants, would be free to worship as long as they did not threaten the security of the kingdom.

Many people lined the streets in joy at the return of the

monarchy, and the beginning of a new era was celebrated with the lavish coronation of the King, known as the 'Merry Monarch', who had spent so many years in exile. However, there was not universal pleasure at Charles's return. There were those who felt nothing but hatred for the Stuarts. Among this group were those Protestants known as Nonconformists, including Presbyterians, Baptists, Congregationalists, Fifth Monarchists and Quakers, who did not wish to conform to the Anglican form of Protestantism. This group, including Blood, would present the newly restored regime with its most enduring challenge.

In May 1661 Charles II opened the new Parliament. The Cavalier Parliament, as it was known, would not be dissolved until 1679. One of the major issues to face the new monarch and his Parliament was that of religion. The Act of Parliament, promised under the Declaration of Breda, that was to ensure 'liberty to tender consciences', or in other words religious toleration, never came into being. Instead, what has often been termed the 'Anglican revenge' was implemented in the form of the Clarendon Code. Just as the Nonconformists had feared, a number of Acts of Parliament were passed that underlined Anglican superiority at the expense of the other Protestant denominations. One of those most responsible for this so-called 'Anglican revenge' was the Bishop of London, and Archbishop of Canterbury from 1663, Gilbert Sheldon. He was principal among those who successfully pushed for this dominance of the episcopal church.

As Charles was always more concerned with loyalty to the Crown than religious observance, he personally favoured toleration for both Protestant Nonconformists and Roman Catholics. However, the atmosphere created by the Clarendon Code was rife with dangerous religious dissent and plots. In general, Protestant fears of a bloody Roman Catholic insurrection had never really gone away since Guy Fawkes and the Gunpowder Plot of 1605. Although there was no other real Roman Catholic plot during the seventeenth century, Protestants were obsessively frightened and ready to accept any patched-up story of Roman Catholics preparing to take over the kingdom. Such an atmosphere later played perfectly into the hands of the political schemer and religious fanatic Titus Oates in 1678.[2]

Charles was also aware that dissatisfaction with his regime was prevalent among a radical group within the Protestant Nonconformist community, and that they posed a very serious threat of insurrection. It was not only the men of violence who were a problem but also the clergy who encouraged their congregations by preaching seditious sermons. Stories of Protestant plots abounded and throughout the 1660s there were many arrests and interrogations.

The potential of these groups for causing trouble was amply demonstrated in 1661 when those known as the Fifth Monarchists led by Thomas Venner began an insurrection that disrupted London for three days. The Fifth Monarchists were an extreme millenarian sect devoted to bringing about their version of heaven on earth through violence. Fourteen of their heads were subsequently placed on London Bridge as an example to those who were considering similar actions. Venner's Rising, as it became known, resulted in a clamp-down on meetings of Nonconformists of all types and the arrest of many, including Quakers and Baptists as well as Fifth Monarchists. The result of all this was to force these groups to operate 'underground' and to strengthen the principles of their most extreme elements.

The traditional religion of the Blood family was Presbyterianism. Presbyterians formed one of the largest and consequently most dominant of these Nonconformist Protestant groups. One of the Reformed Churches, Presbyterianism derived from the teachings of John Calvin, who was born in northern France in 1509. Calvin became converted to Protestantism and went on to develop his own theology, which he put into effect in the city-state of Geneva. He was particularly noted for his attacks on

Roman Catholicism and the Pope. His most famous treatise is *Instruction in the Christian Religion*, known as the *Institutes*, the first edition of which appeared in 1536 and the final version in 1559. It was a work he described himself as the 'sum of Piety'. In England Calvinist doctrines took the form of Puritanism, while in Scotland and Ireland they developed into Presbyterianism.

In line with Calvinist belief the Presbyterians placed a major emphasis upon the 'word of God', i.e. the scriptures. Predestination, by which certain people known as the Elect were to be 'saved' and the rest 'damned', was also central to their beliefs. Under their system of church government they opposed any kind of hierarchy such as the episcopalianism of the Roman Catholic and Anglican Churches. All their ministers were regarded as equal in status, and decisions were made by ministers and elders elected from among the congregation.

Presbyterianism developed into the state church in Scotland but in England the story was very different. Queen Elizabeth had opposed all attempts to make the Protestant Church of England a Presbyterian church. James I was just as determined to block its advancement, as he particularly disliked the Presbyterian view that in the eyes of God the King was not an authority over the church but in fact had a duty to support it. With Charles I came the implementation of Archbishop Laud's anti-Presbyterian and anti-Puritan measures in favour of Anglicanism.

The Presbyterians were committed to what for them were two seminal documents, the National Covenant signed in 1638 and the Solemn League and Covenant signed in 1643. Under the National Covenant they showed their conviction to fight the Anglican measures being introduced by Archbishop Laud and under the Solemn League and Covenant they pledged their support for Parliament against the King in return for the establishment of the Presbyterian church in England.

When presented with the challenge of the Restoration

and subsequent religious circumstances many Presbyterians were not prepared to take any part in armed resistance, but there was a sizeable group who felt otherwise.

In Ireland Charles was faced with a particularly troublesome and combative religious mix. Apart from the majority Roman Catholic community there were the Protestants, consisting of Church of Ireland Anglicans and, just as in England and Scotland, the Nonconformists. The Presbyterian population in Ireland was concentrated in Ulster. They had come, the majority from Scotland and some from England, mostly as a result of the plantation policy. Some, mainly English Presbyterian families such as the Bloods, had settled outside Ulster. The years of Cromwell's supremacy had been good to people like the Bloods. They had property, wealth and standing in the community. If things had stayed thus, Blood might well have lived out a quiet, contented life as a country gentleman and never have come under the gaze of history.

The militants from within the Nonconformist community who were prepared to take up arms for their religion were commonly referred to as 'phanaticks'. Since they were drawn from all the Nonconformist traditions they were weakened by the disparate nature of their backgrounds and the fact that they never worked as well together as they should have.

After the Restoration, and as a result of his diminished position in society, Blood was one of those who became more and more associated with the determined people within Presbyterianism who were willing to use violence to fight for their religious rights. This dedication to the cause of Protestant Nonconformity became the driving force of his life.

The strength of Blood's personal religious convictions can be gleaned from a small pocketbook found on his person when he was arrested in 1671. Although the original is lost, a copy of the book's contents survives.[3] In this pocketbook he had written down seventy 'deliverences since I was for ye lord's cause', which is a list of a number of occasions on which he believed that he had escaped arrest or death only because he was doing God's work. The 'deliverences', although undated, run in a chronological order from 1663 to 1671 and the entries demonstrate his belief in the justice of his cause and in divine providence.

In this pocketbook he also noted down twenty-two of his moral and religious precepts. These are rules by which he wanted to live his life and as such are a valuable insight into his personal religious values. It is true that these rules may be more aspirational than actually descriptive of the way he lived his life, in a sense more of a resolution list, but they do portray his religious priorities. They once again show how a firm belief in providence and a strong faith in God drove him in his actions. Blood states this commitment to God clearly when he writes that he would not 'forsake ye cause of God for any difficu[lties] . . . and to count nothing too deare to forsake'. He also wants to be every day 'in serious consideration of . . . Christ and what he hath done'. He does not want to be 'slothfull in ye works of ye Lord'.[4]

The acts he does are done for the Lord and not for any gain on his own behalf. It is clear that his motivation is very different from that of a common criminal. He does not 'desire highest glory . . . but rather to desire a middle condition in my world . . . not . . . to make great myself or family by my cause but content with a comfortable condition except by god's blessing on my industry . . . Not to boast of my self . . .'.[5]

Although he breaks the laws of the land, he is content that what he is doing is justified as a part of God's plan. For him there is a clear distinction between what he does for his religion and what those involved in ordinary criminality do. This is clearly demonstrated in the pocketbook by his description of the actions of his son, who became a highwayman, as 'my son's wickedness'. It is clear that Blood's own actions are motivated by a deep religious conviction. His belief in divine providence is illustrated by the entry: 'To labour to be content with my condition considering nothing coming by chance.'[6]

On a practical level he writes of not wanting to break engagements and also avoiding 'wine and strong drink' as well as 'excess in . . . recreations, . . . pomp, or . . . apparale'. The reference to strong drink and wine may have been more aspirational than the others, as a government official would later refer to the fact that Blood's head could be easily turned by 'wine and treats'.[7] Blood also expresses a desire to shun any 'quibling or jokeing' and '. . . all obsene & scurulous talke'. Instead, he urges himself to 'promote profitable discourse'.[8]

It was with this kind of fundamentalist religious fervour that Blood was observing events as they unfolded following the restoration of the Stuart monarchy. The Anglicans were once again in the ascendant and the new Anglican Church of England did not look kindly on Roman Catholics nor on Protestant Nonconformists. Blood, as a committed Nonconformist and having also been a Cromwellian soldier, found himself in a most precarious position. It can be argued that the unfolding of political events transformed him into what has been termed 'a brave man on the wrong side of politics and society'.[9]

Two major issues of concern to all those in Blood's position at the time were the questions of land ownership in Ireland and religious toleration of Nonconformity. Undoubtedly land ownership in Ireland was a major problem in the wake of Cromwell. Ireland was left with the disastrous legacy of a number of opposing factions all coveting the same land. It was going to be a difficult problem for anyone to solve and it would be impossible to satisfy everyone. The King had to consider both those dispossessed people who had supported his father and himself through the war and had spent those years of exile with him, and those who were in actual possession of the land and without whom his restoration would not have taken place.

Among those parties claiming land were the 'adventurers' who had been pledged forfeited land by Charles I in return for the money they put forward to aid the war effort, the Confederate Catholics with whom Charles had made a solemn treaty and the soldiers of the Commonwealth army whose arrears of pay he had undertaken to discharge. There were the so-called ''49 officers' who had served the monarchy in the Irish rebellion since the beginning of 1649, and the Irish Catholics who had followed the King into Flanders. Then there were also those unfortunate Roman Catholics who, although declared innocent of involvement in rebellion, had been taken from their land and transplanted west of the Shannon by Cromwell.[10] With the inevitable violence beginning to break out over the issue, Charles decided that all adventurers and settlers should retain their land for now until the matter could be dealt with more fully by means of legislation.

On 30 November 1660 a formula for land settlement was introduced in the form of the Gracious Declaration. Under the provisions of this declaration the Protestant adventurers and soldiers were to keep the land they held on 7 May 1659. However, all the land held by the Church in 1641 was to be restored and those dispossessed Roman Catholics who could prove that they had played no part in the rebellion, termed 'Innocents', were also to be restored to their land provided that enough land was found to compensate those who had bought their estates. Overall, at this stage, it was a settlement that pleased the Protestants by proposing for the most part a confirmation of the existing situation. However, the major flaw in the plan was that there was never going to be enough land in Ireland to satisfy all needs!

This complex problem still needed to be tackled on a more long-term basis. As has been said, 'no more perplexing problem faced the restored Stuart monarchy than that of an Irish settlement'.[11] The King knew that it was to be no easy task in the volatile political climate of Ireland and on 4 November 1661 he appointed the 1st Duke of Ormonde as Lord Lieutenant of Ireland. Ormonde was well aware that it would be a difficult appointment and that the questions of land and religion were to be among his greatest problems. He expressed his reservations about the problems that lay ahead to a friend at the time:

> In that employment, besides many other unpleasant difficulties, there are two disadvantages proper to me; one of the contending parties believing I owe them more kindness and protection than I can find myself chargeable with; and the other suspecting I retain that prejudice to them which I am as free from. This temper in them will be attended undeniably with clamour and scandal upon my most equal and wary deportment.[12]

Ormonde also writes in a letter of the time to his wife's friend Dr Fennell, referring to the treatment of what he calls the ancient natives under the Gracious Declaration, that 'I am not afraid to say that I am sorry for them . . .'.[13] However, most of his sympathy lay with the old English Roman Catholic families who had been dispossessed.[14] But, whatever his personal feelings, he was now Lord Lieutenant of the country and faced with the duty of finding a solution to this most intractable problem.

The Commissioners of the first Court of Claims, who had been appointed to implement the Declaration and make a judgment on each individual claim for land, had during their first session declared innocent thirty-eight out of forty-five Roman Catholics. In 1662 the Act of Settlement was given the royal assent and the following year seven commissioners began the work of the second Court of Claims. In an effort to alleviate Protestant fears over the first Court, the commissioners appointed to the new Court of Claims were all English-born gentlemen. This time in eight months they found 707 claimants to be 'innocent', including 566 Roman Catholics, all of whom were to be restored to their land.[15]

With these kinds of results shock and anger about the work of the Court soon spread in the Protestant community. They complained about what they perceived as a generous policy being applied to Roman Catholics and began exerting pressure at influential levels within the Establishment. They were resisted, however, by both Ormonde and the King. Sir Audley Mervyn, one of those leading the discontent, warned Ormonde that 'alarm that Hannibal was at the gates, was hot throughout the Protestant Plantations'.[16] The Irish House of Commons, consisting mostly of Protestant settlers, wanted Ormonde to change the rules to make the restoration of Roman Catholics to their land much more difficult. They passed a resolution 'pledging themselves to do their utmost to prevent the great and manifold prejudices and inconveniences which threatened the Protestants of Ireland from the Court of Claims'. It was the type of language that only served to encourage those, like Blood, who were ready to take up arms for the Protestant cause.

Aside from land, the other fundamental issue of concern to Blood and the Protestant Nonconformist community was toleration for their religious beliefs and practices. As we have seen, even though Charles had signed up to the Covenants during his time in exile, once the monarchy was restored he made the Anglican (episcopalian) Church the established church once again. In Ireland this re-established church was put under the control of the Archbishop of Armagh and Primate of Ireland, John Bramhall.

As events developed, those who refused to conform to the Anglican Church were being put under more and more pressure. As part of the Clarendon Code the Act of Uniformity was passed in all three kingdoms in 1662. Any minister of religion who did not testify his acceptance of the Book of Common Prayer and renounce the Solemn League and Covenant was to be 'deprived' of his ministry.

Thousands of Nonconformist ministers in Ireland fell victim to this particular piece of repressive legislation in what became known as the Great Ejection. It was a development that was deeply repugnant to radical Nonconformist 'phanaticks' like Blood.

Those primarily concerned with politics, such as Charles himself and Ormonde, were for the most part willing to tolerate the Non-conformists as long as they did not threaten the stability of the kingdom. In fact Charles promised a group of Ulster ministers, when they came to see him, 'protection for their separate religious meetings if they could not accept the episcopalian Church'.[17] Charles even proposed a Declaration of Indulgence, which would have exempted certain people from the full effects of the Act of Uniformity. However, many, including clerics of the established church who had themselves suffered persecution under Cromwell, were far less tolerant. Much to his annoyance the King failed to get his Declaration through the House of Lords and the majority wanted all Nonconformist activity firmly suppressed.

Blood and others who felt like him had now reached the point where they were prepared to use armed insurrection to fight for their religious beliefs and property rights. They came to the conclusion that such action was the only way to bring attention to their cause. By this time Blood probably believed that his own lands were likely to be confiscated. Thus it was that his life took a sudden and profound turn and a Protestant rebel of great guile and cunning was created.

4

BLOOD'S PLOT

The year was 1663 and a radical group of Protestant Nonconformists had decided to target both Dublin Castle and the person of the new Lord Lieutenant of Ireland. The Castle and the Duke of Ormonde were chosen because of their significance as symbolic representations of royal authority in Ireland. The plot was to take place as part of a wider revolt involving uprisings on both sides of the Irish Sea. This planned action of the Protestant Nonconformists, later known as Blood's Plot, was to transform Blood from a figure of relative obscurity into a 'most wanted' man. It would also change his life fundamentally. The authorities would later form the opinion that not only was he instrumental in devising the plot, but also that he authored the declaration in which the participants outlined their various demands. At least one seized copy of that declaration was found to have been written in his own hand-writing.[1] He was believed to be, as it has been put, 'the soul of the insurrectionary movement'.[2]

The demands of these Nonconformists were that all the English would be restored to the land they held at the end of the Cromwellian era, that all soldiers involved would have the arrears owed to them paid in full at once, that the Solemn League and Covenant would be

29

enforced and that, as they stated it themselves, 'no popery would be tolerated'.[3]

Also involved in Blood's Plot was his relative the Revd William Lecky, a Presbyterian clergyman. Lecky, from County Westmeath, had been educated at Trinity College in Dublin and spent some time as a minister in County Meath.[4] Around Christmas 1662 Blood and Lecky had paid a visit to Ulster together in order to drum up Scottish support for the plot; however, they achieved only limited success.

Undoubtedly the whole affair had the hallmark of Blood's daring character in both its audacity and simplicity. Between 6 and 7 on the morning in question a small group of six men were to enter Dublin Castle by the Great Gate and make their way to the back entrance on Ship Street, where they would join the petitioners who would be waiting to see the Lord Lieutenant. A tradition at that time held that anyone who wished to petition the Lord Lieutenant personally was entitled to come to the Castle to do so. Meanwhile, the bulk of the rebels, numbering around eighty men, would remain outside the gates. Once Ormonde had arrived, a man disguised as a baker was to cause a diversion by dropping a basket of loaves at the back gate. As the guards began helping this 'unfortunate' man to pick up his loaves the small group would attack and disarm them. The others would then be let in through the gates and, with the assistance of men on horseback, the Castle would be taken and the Lord Lieutenant captured. Once the Castle was secure the horsemen would advance on the city of Dublin itself. The cry 'A free Parliament and an English interest' would be let out.[5]

However, before the plot could be put to the test, a common occurrence of seventeenth-century life intervened when one of their number turned informer. Unknown to Blood and the other plotters, a man called Philip Alden, a former Cromwellian who was a lawyer and dealer in forfeited estates, had kept the Lord Lieutenant informed of developments almost from the beginning. He had first unburdened himself to his employer, Colonel Edward Vernon, who then brought him before the Duke to tell the whole story. Ormonde decided that the best course of action was for Alden to continue associating with the plotters while security would be increased at the Castle. Then it was a question of waiting for the right time to strike against the 'phanaticks'.

In addition to this treachery, the plotters seem to have struck themselves a severe blow when Colonel Alexander Jephson, MP for Trim in County Meath, was given the task of attempting to recruit one Sir Theophilus Jones to the cause.[6] According to Jones's own record of the event Jephson approached him at Lucan, five miles from Dublin, on Tuesday 19 May 1663. Jones was accompanied at the time by a Colonel Jeofferies. After they had greeted each other, Jeofferies left the others to go to attend to his troop of soldiers. Once he and Jones were alone, Jephson began to refer to the Court of Claims and what he perceived as the unfair treatment being handed out to those he termed 'the English'. He said that he never observed 'so generall a discontent among the English as at present by reason of those proceedings; and that it was not possible that the English should long beare it'.

He then asked Jones if he had seen half a dozen horsemen pass that way earlier in the day, saying that they were some of his. Jones said he had not seen them but that they could well have passed by without him noticing. Jephson then said that he must leave soon because he had a trial to attend at the Court of Claims in Dublin on Thursday. However, Jones had noticed that Jephson's horse had thrown a shoe and told him that he should first have that attended to. One of Jones's servants brought Jephson's horse to the forge to have it reshod.

While the horse was being attended to, Jones, Jephson and Jeofferies walked towards Jones's house. On their way the men engaged in idle chat, with Jephson enquiring after Jones's wife and children. It was when they reached the house that Jephson asked to speak with Jones privately. In order to facilitate this request, Jones asked Jeofferies to go in and told him that they would join him shortly. As Jones and Jephson entered the house, from the hall Jephson noticed some preparations for dinner and informed Jones that he could not dine with them. He asked, however, that they retire to some room wherein they could have their private chat. Jones led him into the buttery and sent for a tankard of ale, a bottle of cider and a dish of meat.

Jephson then turned to what was to be the purpose of their conversation. He began by making a rather leading statement to Jones: 'I know you love the English.' He then informed him that if he could be assured of his secrecy he would tell him something that was 'for the good of the English and the preservation of the English interest'. For the purpose of drawing information from him Jones assured him a number of times of his discretion in such matters. Jephson, perhaps not fully convinced, warned him: 'if you bringe me before the Counsell board, I will denie every thing and criminat you and make you black enough; and much more to that purpose'. Jones attempted to allay his worries by telling him that he had no need to fear any such occurrence.

With that, Jephson laid his hand on a large sword that was at his side, saying that it was a sword he had not worn for thirteen years. He told Jones that his will was made, he had said goodbye to his wife and thirteen children, and 'hee and many more were resolved to adventure theire lives'.

He then proceeded to discuss the details of the proposed plot, during which he expressed the rather fanciful hope that they would seize the castles of Dublin, Cork, Limerick, Waterford and Clonmel. They had, according to him, '1,000 horse in Dublin for the secureing of the city'. They also, he claimed, had sufficient money to pay off the arrears of all those members of the army who took part. He spoke of his belief that some of this money was to come from Holland. He told Jones that the Duke of Ormonde was to be seized but treated civilly. Many thousands of copies of their Declaration were printed and ready to be distributed. Jephson concluded by informing Jones that he was soon to be offered command of an army of 20,000 men and that he would be wise not to refuse it. Having made these shocking revelations, Jephson left for Dublin.

Either Jephson was seriously deluded as to the potential scale of the uprising or he was intentionally trying to overrate it merely to enlist Jones's support for the cause. The spy Philip Alden informed Ormonde that Jephson was very pleased with how the discussion had gone and told his comrades how confident he was of having managed to enlist Jones in the upcoming struggle.[7] In reality Jones had no intention of joining the plotters and all Jephson had managed to do was to damage their chances of success even more. In fact Jones wrote the whole account down and relayed it directly to the Duke of Ormonde the following morning.

After a number of date changes, the eve of the rising finally arrived. Those involved held prayer meetings at three different venues that day in order to plead for divine assistance.[8] Reflecting their different hues of Protestantism, two Presbyterian gatherings took place and one Congregationalist. That night Blood met with William Lecky, Alexander Jephson, James Tanner, a former clerk to Henry Cromwell's secretary, Richard Thompson, the deputy Provost-Marshal of Leinster, and others at the White Hart Inn in Patrick Street, Dublin. Things became very dangerous, however, when the landlady became worried about such a large number of clearly agitated men gathering, and warned them that if they did not leave her establishment immediately she would inform the Lord Lieutenant of their meeting.[9] Ormonde did not need her information as Philip Alden was also there that night.

Although Colonel Jephson had told Jones that they had a

thousand horse at their disposal in Dublin and that Sir
Henry Ingoldesby, the former Governor of Limerick, would
be supporting them with another thousand, the actual
numbers involved were small. It appears that when
William Skelton arrived in support with six horse it was
noted that he brought the number available to only ten![10]
Realising that they were somewhat short of numbers, the
insurrection was postponed once again to await the arrival
of an expected 500 men in a week.

Although he was informed of this postponement,
Ormonde decided that the time was now right for him to
move against the plotters. A declaration was drawn up by
him and his Council, dated 21 May 1663, and sent to
significant people in the kingdom:

> . . . certain wicked persons of fanatick and disloyal
> principles, dis-affected to his majesties just and gracious
> government, and the peace and settlement of this
> kingdom, have lately most traiterously and disloyally
> conspired to raise rebellious disturbances in this realm,
> and particularly had designed on the 21 day of this
> present May to surprize and take his Majesties Castle of
> Dublin, his principal fort in his kingdom, and to seize on
> . . . the Lord Lieutenant . . .[11]

The call was sent out for anyone who might be involved to be
arrested.

Two days later another declaration was issued
announcing the names of the conspirators who had been
arrested:

Thomas Scot	Andrew Sturges
Colonel Edward Warren	William Dod
Theophilus Sandford	Stephen Radford
John Chambers	Abraham Langton
Alexander Jephson	Wiliam Bayly
Philip Alden	Robert Davies

Richard Thompson	John Biddel
John Fouke	John Smullen
Edward Baines	Thomas Ball
William Lackey	John Griffin
Thomas Boyd	William Bradford
James Tanner	Samuel Fann

Some time later Major Henry Jones and Richard Price were also apprehended.[12]

Another declaration made it clear, however, that many others 'had found means to escape, and are not as yet apprehended'. The first of these missing people to be named was 'Thomas Blood, late of Sarny near Dunboine in the County of Meath'.[13] This declaration demanded that Blood and the others give themselves up within forty-eight hours; any who did not were declared 'to be rebels and traitors against His Majesty, His Crown and Dignity, and to be accordingly prosecuted by all His Majesties good subjects'.[14] A significant reward was also offered for their capture:

> . . . any person or persons that shall apprehend the said Thomas Blood . . . or any of them, and bring him or them, or cause him or them to be brought to the High Sheriff of the County wherein he or they shall be apprehended, at, by or before the 24th day of June next, shall have as a reward for the said service, the sum of one hundred pounds . . .[15]

During the investigation before Ormonde, one James Tanner gave rather damning evidence against Blood.[16] He said that the first time he had heard of the intended plot was from Blood in early April, when he met him in the street. Blood had shown him a letter, which Tanner thought suggested that Henry Cromwell was willing to become involved in the struggle. Blood told him that he intended to take Dublin Castle in May and that the Scots were to rise also.

Tanner also testified that a copy of the declaration which was shown to him was in Blood's own handwriting. It was a handwriting he professed to be very familiar with. He also gave evidence of having dined with Blood, Blood's relative Lecky and others at the White Hart on St Patrick's Street, Dublin, on 21 May. Tanner also stated that he had been at Blood's lodging at the Bottle near St Patrick's Gate.

By June the number arrested had risen to seventy. At the trial of those accused, when passing sentence Judge James Barry said that he was very sorry to see persons of their quality stand in that place and described their plot as 'a sin against all mankind'.[17] Alexander Jephson, Richard Thompson and Edward Warren were all sentenced to hang for their part in the plot.

Public interest in the plot was shown by the large crowd that assembled on the day of the executions. At one point the masses became alarmed and stampeded. Once order was restored, Colonel Jephson in his final confession tried to lay the blame for his involvement upon the Roman Catholics, while Thompson claimed that he had been 'drawn in' by Blood.[18] Since Thompson used the opportunity of his last speech to offer his loyalty to both the King and the Church of England, he was not beheaded after death like the other two.[19]

The House of Commons in Ireland, where Blood's grandfather had once sat proudly as a Member, condemned Blood's Plot at its next meeting in October 1665. The journal of the House states:

> The House being sat, they fell into debate of the heinousness of the plot, contrived against his Majesty and Government, within this Kingdom of Ireland, which was to have been put in execution about the latter end of May, one thousand six hundred and sixty three, had not the same, by the mercy of God, and blessing given to the vigilant endeavours of his Grace the Lord Lieutenant, been discovered.[20]

The House also declared its intention to 'make inspection into such of their Members, as had a hand in the said wicked plot'.[21] In fact, apart from Jephson, who was an MP, seven other members of the House were found to be implicated in the plot: Robert Shapcote, John Chambers, Thomas Boyd, Alexander Staples, Abel Warren, John Ruxton and Thomas Scott.[22] Those Members were all expelled and declared incapable of sitting in any future Parliament. The House also applied to the Lord Lieutenant that the offenders be 'made uncapable of exercising any employment civil, military, or ecclesiastical, within this Kingdom'.[23]

The version of the declaration written in Blood's own handwriting was read to the House. The Members declared that

> . . . the paper, being an intended declaration, written with the hand of Thomas Blood, late of Sarney, one of the ring-leaders in the said conspiracy . . . is scandalous, treasonable, and false in every particular . . . and therefore that his Grace would be pleased, if he thinks fit, to command the said paper, or a copy thereof, to be burnt by the hand of the common hangman, at the most publick place in this city.[24]

The Revd Lecky would undoubtedly have been sentenced to hang as well but for the fact that he was either driven insane by the experience of his trial, or at least managed to feign insanity. Following various hallucinations in the dock, including one where he announced that he was Jesus Christ, followed by an attempt to kill himself by banging his head repeatedly on the wall of his gaol cell, he was reprieved from hanging. After about six months, two accomplices dressed as women, who filed his chains and disguised Lecky in a similar manner, set him free from Newgate prison. We do not know for sure whether one of these 'women' was in fact Blood although it is possible. But whoever they were they made the bad mistake of splitting from him in Little Thomas Court, leaving the bewildered man to fend for himself. For some reason the Revd Lecky decided to ask a passing servant for the loan of a ladder, whereupon the bemused boy fetched his master, to whom Lecky confessed his identity and asked for assistance. Not surprisingly the Reverend soon found himself back in captivity and this time could not escape the ultimate punishment.

On the morning of his hanging, as a large crowd of perhaps over two thousand[25] gathered to watch the event, a rumour began to spread among the spectators to the effect that Thomas Blood was on his way to free his relative. Such was Blood's growing reputation by this time that the crowd, fearing for their lives, panicked and fled, as did the hangman. Unfortunately for Lecky the rumour proved to be false and the hangman later returned to carry out his duty.[26]

In order to preserve his cover the spy Philip Alden also had to be arrested with the others. Once the executions had taken place his 'escape' from gaol was carefully orchestrated. He was later brought to England, where he was introduced to both the King and the Lord Chancellor. He went on to work as a spy for the next three years. When his cover was finally in danger of being blown he retired in Ireland with a formal pardon and a pension of £100 a year, although, as was commonly the case, it appears that his pension was often in arrears.[27]

Although some writers have doubted the leadership role played by Blood in this plot,[28] Ormonde seems to have been in no doubt on the matter. He wrote much later, in 1678, that 'the plot then laid for the surprise of this castle was contrived and near brought to execution by Thomas Blood and others of his crew'[29] and, in 1679, that 'Mr. Blood's Plot was on foot and brought near to execution'.[30]

Although it turned out to be a military non-event, there is no doubt that the plot had an influence on political events in Ireland, focusing the attention of the government on the dangerous dissatisfaction of Protestants over the question of land ownership, and convincing them that changes were needed to the work of the Court of Claims. So much so, in fact, that the commissioners of the Court of Claims felt themselves under huge pressure in the wake of it. One of them, Winston Churchill, complained that they were being blamed for Blood's Plot 'as if we were more in fault for doing justice that they for opposing it'.[31]

One result was the Act of Explanation, which passed through the Irish Parliament in 1665. This Act favoured the Protestants in the question of land ownership and left them in a clearly dominant position in Ireland. Under its terms there was no provision for a resumption of the hearings on claims of innocence, which meant that those Roman Catholics who had not already been judged innocent of the rebellion of 1641 had now lost their land permanently. Ormonde said that the Explanatory Act was the most favourable measure for the 'English interest that could either with honesty or modesty be contrived'.[32]

However, on that second great issue of seventeenth-century Ireland, the question of religious toleration for Nonconformists, Blood's Plot could be said to have been anything but helpful. In fact it allowed those of the Established Church to point to the plot as proof that the Nonconformists constituted a real threat to the security of the kingdom. As a result, warrants for the arrest of at least forty Nonconformist ministers were issued, forcing many of them into hiding.[33] There was also added pressure for religious conformity throughout the country. But though at first Ormonde 'savagely harried the dissenters, driving many ministers abroad',[34] after some time he decided that to continue investigating Blood's Plot in this way was not only futile but also counter-productive and so eased off.[35] He wrote to the Earl of Anglesey on the issue in 1678:

Upon the examination of several persons, I found the design was too far spread to ravel any further into it, and that if I should follow the thread of the discovery as far it might lead me, possibly I might bring on that insurrection and rebellion which they designed, and I had rather should be prevented than punished.[36]

5

ON THE RUN

After the discovery of the plot in Dublin, Blood, once a respected man of property and rank under the Cromwellian regime, now found himself an outlaw with a price of £100 on his head. As he was forced to travel in disguise at grave personal risk, he moved ever deeper into the ranks of the radicals, among whom he became a significant figure. A government intelligence note from 1663 speaks of the rebels as saying that their 'King', meaning God, 'will overcome with Blood'.[1] He and people like him did their best to become a thorn in the side of the authorities as they posed a constant and realistic threat of insurrection. Every rumour of a potential plot by them had to be taken seriously and monitored very carefully by the government. During these difficult times Maria decided to go back to Holcroft Hall with their son Thomas and their first daughter, who had been born in Ireland.

Amusingly, while Blood was concerned with such important events, his name appears in the records in connection with a matter of relatively less importance. In June 1663 a butcher named Richard Dolman from Dublin petitioned the Duke of Ormonde for the return of a cow, which he claimed had been stolen from him by Blood. In his petition Dolman claimed that he had sold a bull to Thomas Blood. Some months later he sent his cow, who was the 'mother' of the bull in question, to graze with him. When it was time for him to kill the cow he sent his servant to collect her. His servant met with Lecky, who sent one of Blood's servants to fetch the bull and cow, whereupon both animals were brought to Dolman's house in Dublin. Up to this point all was fine and legitimate, but things turned nasty when later both the bull and cow went missing. Dolman had in his possession a certificate to prove that the cow in question was legally his and he claimed that it had been stolen by Blood. He requested that the Duke have the cow returned to him, he 'being a very poore man'.[2] One has to wonder whether this case was nothing more than an example of someone trying to take advantage of the difficult situation in which Blood now found himself. We do not know if the bovines in question were ever actually recovered by Dolman or if they proved as elusive as the man accused of their theft.

While on the run Blood seems to have demonstrated a talent for disguise. He often appeared as a clergyman, and even, amazingly for an extreme Protestant, as a Catholic priest should the occasion demand it. He was to use the garb of a clergyman to great effect later on when stealing the Crown Jewels. During this period he spent time in various parts of Ireland, including Wicklow and Antrim, where he probably stayed at the so-called 'White House' on Belfast Lough which was occupied by a friend of his called Thomas Boyde.

An insight into the danger under which he was forced to live during these years on the run can be gleaned from the contents of the pocketbook kept by him in which he listed a number of his narrow escapes. The entries made by Blood in this book, although undated, run chronologically and his mention of events like the plague and the fire of London can help us date some of his activities. He writes of his luck in escaping when most were 'taken' after the Dublin Plot and how he actually stayed in the city for three days. He also mentions his various escapes from enemies as diverse as false brethren and on one particular occasion dogs! He also mentions being able to board a ship without being recognised but how when he arrived at his destination there were many who could have identified him on shore.

During these years Blood, while constantly on the move, was involved in a succession of plots against the government. From the State Papers for the period and the contents of his pocketbook we can piece together at least some of his activities during these years.[3] The potential threat posed by him during this time is illustrated by the fact that when as powerful a person as the Duke of Ormonde was planning to pay a visit to his house in Dunmore near Kilkenny he was warned to be careful as Blood was roaming the countryside.[4]

After the failure of the plot in Dublin, Blood went to England, where he soon became involved in another plot against the government. He was one of those on a rebel council, along with another activist called John Mason, which planned a rising in the North of England in 1663. In the end the rising failed when the group was once again betrayed by one of its own members; a man called John Atkinson gave information on the leaders to the authorities.[5]

After the Northern Plot was broken up in the autumn of 1663, Blood seems to have paid a short visit to Holland. Not long after this he was back in England once again and in 1664 was involved with a rebel group planning to attack the Tower of London and Whitehall, and also to murder the King, the Duke of York and others.[6] Perhaps it was at this time that Blood first became aware of the security limitations of the Tower of London. In a plan similar to the one he would later use to rob the Crown Jewels, the rebels planned to gain entry to the Tower on the apparently innocent pretext of wishing to see the armoury.[7] The group once again included John Mason, and a number of that extreme Protestant religious sect, the Fifth Monarchists, who had unsuccessfully opposed the government in 1661. Blood and his colleagues were also in contact with rebels in Scotland. They held at least one meeting at a widow's house in Petty France. Although the government was once again aware of their activities, through informers such as John Atkinson who had infiltrated the group, their attempts to arrest the 'phanaticks' ultimately failed.[8] But they did manage to prevent the rising from taking place.

This was just one example of how involved with the Fifth Monarchists Blood became at this time. Although one could never have described him as a committed Fifth Monarchist, he does seem to have become a very prominent member of their group, describing them as 'a bold and daring sort of people like himself'.[9] He even became a leader in the group and was responsible for putting some members under court martial, charged with the betrayal of secrets to the authorities. This court martial was held in a tavern and those charged were found guilty and sentenced to be shot within two days.[10] However, when the hour of execution arrived, Blood used his power at the last moment to spare their lives. He then told them, rather ironically as future events would turn out, 'to go to their new master [Charles II], tell him all that had happened, and request him, in the name of their old confederates, to be as favourable to such of them as should at any time stand in need of his mercy'.[11]

From the evidence of his pocketbook Blood seems to have managed to survive unscathed in London during the worst period of the plague in 1665, which is reputed to have killed more than 75,000 people. As victims lay dying all around him in the London streets, and the horrible sight of rotting corpses was to be seen in the fields, in his pocketbook Blood attributes his survival 'from ye pestilence' to God's blessings on his activities.[12]

The government also became aware that Blood was involved in a plot being organised in the house of one Captain Browne in Liverpool in late 1665 and early 1666.[13] Browne had been one of those involved in Blood's Plot in

Dublin.[14] As England was involved in the Second Dutch War at the time, the rebels decided that an ideal time to strike would be as soon as England was defeated in a major naval battle. They entertained high hopes of receiving money, armaments and troops from the Dutch.[15] Blood went to Dublin with another member of the group, George Ayres, to meet with their fellow radicals there' at the house of a brewer called Cooke.[16] The plan on that side of the Irish Sea consisted once again of attacking and taking Dublin Castle, while this time the Duke of Ormonde was to be assassinated. At the same time the rebels in England would march to Scotland to meet supporters there.[17] Their lofty aims on this occasion included the abolition of the monarchy, the House of Lords and the Established Church. They planned to restore the Long Parliament, forty members of which they claimed to have among them.

Ormonde actually became aware of this plot as early as February 1666. Captain Robert Oliver in Ireland informed the Duke that his wife had been approached by their friend, Robert Taylor, who it seems in an act of kindness had wanted to prepare them for the rebellion. The Olivers negotiated a security for Taylor's life and property, and he confessed all to the authorities.[18] Unfortunately for the plotters, the informer Philip Alden was also in the thick of things once again. When he became aware of the intended plot and of Blood's involvement, Ormonde told the Secretary of State, Lord Arlington, 'I shall try to arrest him and prevent this mischief.'[19]

As usual, however, intelligence on the exact whereabouts of Blood was sketchy. A note sent to Lord Orrery dated February 1666 stated: 'Captain Blood, who carried on the design in Ireland, may be found at Colonel Gilby Carr's, in the North of Ireland, or at his wife's near Dublin'.[20] In the end the insurrection never took place and Blood, as ever, was not arrested.

As the hunt for Blood proceeded, the authorities suffered a setback in May 1666, when a Fifth Monarchist prisoner named John Patshall escaped from the Gatehouse Gaol. They had regarded him as a potentially valuable source of information on the location of Blood.[21]

As the Second Dutch War continued during 1666, Blood travelled to the continent with John Lockyer in order to enlist that well-known radical in exile, Edmund Ludlow, in brokering a deal with the Franco-Dutch alliance for their assistance. On arrival in the United Provinces, however, both men were arrested on suspicion of being spies. They were eventually freed with the assistance of another exile, Captain John Phelps, who then travelled with Blood to Lausanne, where they met Ludlow. The mission came to nothing, and Blood found himself singularly unimpressed with Ludlow, whom he considered 'very unable for such an employment'.[22]

It is interesting to note the claim made by one contemporary biographer of Blood that while in Holland he became friendly with Admiral De Ruyter.[23] It is claimed that Blood was one of the few to whom De Ruyter gave an account of how he narrowly survived death as a child. The story, as Blood told it, was that De Ruyter's father was a poor man who relied greatly on his two horses. When those horses were taken from him by troops of the Dutch army he and his family faced ruin. Travelling to the army camp and failing to get any satisfaction, he decided to steal his horses back. Before long the troops arrived once again at his house, guessing that it was he who had taken the horses. On failing to find the animals, however, they set fire to the house, with the parents and the future admiral, only a baby, asleep inside. At first the parents ran out of the house in panic but then the mother ran back bravely into the heat and flames to rescue her baby. On finding the child she threw him out of the window on to a sheet below before jumping to safety herself. They all survived the fire, but that is how close to death the famous admiral had come as a child.

Since we are told this was an episode that was 'quite omitted, or else unknown to the Author that published his

Life in Holland',[24] the implication is that De Ruyter told the story only to a few close acquaintances. Blood's biographer tells us that the admiral told the story to Blood, 'whom he was pleased to admit often into his Society'.[25]

All through this time the government had reports of him moving frequently between Ireland and England using aliases such as Allen and Groves. Often the intelligence seems to have been contradictory. In August 1666 information came from a Captain Grice that Blood and others '. . . are gone for Ireland to do mischief'.[26] Secretary of State Arlington had a spy attempting to track his movements through England and Wales, but the intelligence coming back to him was that Blood had not returned to Ireland at that time.[27] The Earl of Orrery also shows his concern in a letter written to Secretary Arlington in September 1666: 'The arrival of Blood and others here at this juncture has made me put all the province on their guard in case of disturbance.'[28]

In September 1666 a fire which broke out at a baker's in Pudding Lane was blown by means of an easterly gale into the city of London. In spite of valiant attempts made by masses of people armed with buckets of water and the demolition of rows of houses, the Great Fire continued its inexorable progress until a substantial portion of the city had been destroyed. Blood, according to his pocketbook, was back in London at the time of the Great Fire and, as he tells us, was grateful to have escaped arrest. Such was his reputation that there were even those who, rather unfairly, attributed the starting of the fire to him![29]

The same year in Scotland the Presbyterian Covenanters rose in armed revolt against Charles in defence of their religious liberties. It was no wonder that the year 1666 took on a religious significance to those 'devoted to apocalyptic considerations' given that the 'number of the beast in the bible is 666'.[30] It was stated by Viscount Conway, working on information received from the King, and also by both Orrery and Arlington, that Blood was there with his co-religionists fighting in the Pentland Rising of November that year.[31] Blood himself refers to 'ye battle' in his pocketbook, as he does 'the retreat' and being 'healed of my wounds'.[32] So although the rebels were defeated and more than 500 lost their lives in that particular rising, Blood once again managed to escape.

Meanwhile, while all this was going on, as Blood was deeply engaged in Nonconformist Protestant plots and on the run from the authorities, a Captain Toby Barnes had begun the process of acquiring his land in counties Meath and Wicklow. The land was confiscated by royal order on the basis of Blood's treason and after a number of petitions was leased to Captain Barnes in 1666. The order from the King to the Lord Lieutenant reads:

> In remembrance of Sir Toby's service to King Charles I and his faithfulness we direct you to take steps for granting him, &c., under the Great Seal a lease at such rent and for such a term as you think fit for the towns and lands of Sarny, Breatowne and Foylestown in the barony of Dunboyne, County Meath, and 500 acres of unprofitable mountain in Glanmalier alias the Glinns, County Wicklow, formerly belonging to Thomas Blood, of Sarny, lately attainted of high treason, to whom the same were granted by letters patent dated 12 June, 1643.[33]

By 1667 there were reports of Blood being in the north of England trying to stir up trouble in Warrington and Manchester, and he was also spotted at the house of a 'rigid Anabaptist' in Westmorland.[34] In February and March new warrants for his arrest were issued.[35] However, undeterred, by the end of the summer he was ready to challenge the authorities once again.

6

A DARING ESCAPE

In the summer of 1667 two prisoners, Captain John Mason and William Leving, were being transported on horseback to the assizes at York.[1] Mason had been arrested for his involvement in plotting against the government in northern England in 1663, a plot in which Blood had also been involved.[2] In July a warrant had been issued for Mason's transfer from the Tower of London to York, where he was to stand trial. He was well aware that the fate awaiting him was probably a sentence of death. Leving, on the other hand, was being transported from Newgate prison to act as a crown witness against a number of rebels. The soldier charged with the responsibility of leading this heavily armed moving party of seven or eight troops was Corporal William Darcy. Darcy knew that Mason had already escaped from custody once before and so was well aware of his responsibility. On their fourth day of travel the group was joined by a barber named Scott, who decided to accompany them so that he could be guaranteed a safe journey home to York.

Unknown to Corporal Darcy, Blood and at least three other armed men lay in wait with the determined intention of setting free their fellow rebel, Captain Mason. With Blood were two other well-known 'phanaticks', Captain John Lockyer and Timothy Butler.[3] As they waited hidden in bushes some distance from the road, one of Blood's men was on look-out duty at the roadside. However, their plans went awry when for some unknown reason their look-out man left his post, and by the time Blood discovered this he was forced to conclude that the prison party had already passed by. They immediately rode on in an attempt to catch up, but on reaching Darrington near Doncaster concluded that their opportunity had passed them by and it was now too late to strike. As they considered the fate of their friend Mason with what must have been heavy hearts, Blood decided that they would have some nourishment and rest before reluctantly returning to London the following morning.

However, events suddenly turned to their advantage when they heard some horses coming to a halt outside the inn. Blood, on taking a casual look out of the window, was stunned to see his friend Mason and the prison party. He now realised he had been mistaken in assuming that their intended victims had passed them by. It seems that as they rode along Mason requested a drink and told Corporal Darcy of an inn that was just ahead. Darcy agreed to the request, no doubt deciding that a little refreshment would help to shorten the trip for everyone. The Corporal was insistent, however, that all but one soldier would remain on horseback and that the drinks would be brought out to them. On seeing this most welcome turn of events, Blood, never a man to turn his back on serendipity, paid his bill with great haste and got his men out of the inn by another door. They scurried silently to their horses and prepared to take advantage of the situation.

As Blood watched events unfold he saw that another welcome advantage of this detour at the inn was the effect it was now having of splitting up the prison party. The first to move off from the inn was Corporal Darcy himself with four soldiers and the two prisoners. A little while later the others followed. Seizing their opportunity, Blood and his men first crept up on and attacked two men at the rear, successfully dismounting and injuring them. Next they intended to deal in a similar fashion with a man who was just ahead, but they failed to reach him before he had caught up with the main party. Blood was now ready for his next move. He made his way around the prison party until he was ahead of them. He then positioned himself and his horse to block their way through a narrow lane between Wentbridge and Darrington.

It was 7 p.m. when Darcy and his men came upon this lone man standing in the lane demanding that they hand over their prisoner. They were ordered to hand him over or else 'they were dead men'.[4] The soldiers thought that he was either a fool or a madman, and shouted at him to get out of their way. They were soon forced to realise, however, as pistol shots rang out, that not only was this 'fool' serious in his intent but he was also not alone. A vicious fight began.

Unfortunately for Blood an ostler at the inn had failed to tighten the girth on his horse properly, with the result that during the fight he fell off three times, and was forced finally to fight on foot. He found himself driven backwards into a courtyard by two of the soldiers. During the struggle one of them shot him in the pistol arm and then threw a pistol at him, hitting him high on the nose between the eyes. In predictable style, however, Blood managed to prevail. He had one of the soldiers on the ground and was about to finish him off when Mason arrived and told him that they could now make good their escape. Mason persuaded him to spare the soldier on the ground, saying that he had been the kindest one to him on the road.

Corporal Darcy had fought bravely during the attack, which he later stated to have lasted for half an hour, although Blood thought it had been two hours.[5] Darcy was injured twice himself, in the hand and the head, and his horse was shot from under him.[6] A number of his men were also left badly injured. Proctor was shot in the body, Knifton in the arm, Lobley in the thigh and Hewet in the back.[7] A surgeon was brought to tend the injured men.

While all this fighting was going on, the other prisoner, William Leving, had slipped away quietly and hidden in a nearby house. He only emerged when it was all over to surrender himself once again to Corporal Darcy. The reason for this was that Leving knew that Blood or Mason would kill him if given the opportunity, as not only was he on his way to act as a crown witness, but he had also recently informed on a rebel group of which they were both members![8] Leving was an informer whose relationship with the authorities had soured of late, forcing him to take up highway robbery, as a result of which he had been arrested.

When Justice Stringer arrived on the scene Leving furnished him with information on the attackers.[9] He also advised the authorities that people who could recognise Blood and the others should be placed on the outskirts of London, as he believed that they would head for the city.

Darcy left his injured men behind and continued the journey to York to deliver Leving, who might have been wiser to have taken his chances on escaping that day. He was later found dead in his cell, believed to have been poisoned by those he had betrayed.[10] A letter, probably forged, was found on him seeking to exonerate some of those his evidence had placed on the wanted list.[11]

Meanwhile Blood, his men and Mason all made good their escape. Blood was quite badly wounded in the fight and had to ride all that night with 'nothing but blood and gore all over from Top to Toe'.[12] He was forced to take some time to recuperate in the house of a friend in Yorkshire, where he was attended to by a surgeon.[13] Once Leving had furnished the government with the outlaws' names, they realised that their prison party had been set upon by the elusive Thomas Blood.[14] Blood, Mason, Lockyer and Butler all found themselves named in a proclamation published by the King and had a reward of £100 placed upon their heads.

By the King.

A Proclamation for the Discovery and Apprehension of John Lockier, Timothy Butler, Thomas Blood, commonly called Captain Blood, John Mason, and others.

Charles R.

Whereas we have been informed, that the said John Lockier, Timothy Butler, and Captain Blood, with several other persons did lately in most riotous and rebellious manner, at Darrington near Went-bridge in the County of York, violently set upon and assault the guard intrusted with the care of conducting one John Mason, a prisoner for treason, from Our Tower of London to Our city of York, in order to his tryal there; and they having killed and desperately wounded several of the said guard, and others, did rescue and carry away the said Mason, and do lurk in secret places, and not submit themselves to justice; We therefore have thought fit (with the advice of Our Privy Council) to publish this Our Royal Proclamation, and do hereby straitly charge and command all and singular Lords Lieutenants, Deputy-Lieutenants, Justices of the Peace, Mayors, Sheriffs, Bayliffs, and other Our Officers, Ministers, and Subjects whatsoever, to be diligent and use their best endeavours to search for and apprehend the said Lockier, Butler, Blood, and Mason, and all others who were any way instrumental in the said rescue or escape . . . We do hereby further declare, that one hundred pounds sterling shall be given and paid by us to any person or persons, as a recompence for their service, who shall apprehend and bring in the said Lockier, Butler, Blood, and Mason, or any of them, or any other who were their accomplices in the said rescue . . .[15]

They were not captured and three years later Mason turned up as a tavern-keeper in London where he continued his plotting habits. As for Blood, after this latest crime he was wanted by the authorities more than ever.

Nothing much was heard of him for three years and for a time it was even reported that he was dead. One spy called William Freer reported as much to the authorities in September 1667.[16] That particular piece of misinformation could have been initially circulated by Blood himself. Or perhaps it sprang from the fact that he had been quite badly wounded in the Mason escape.

In fact, the truth is rather stranger. It was during this period that the Blood family turned their attention to the worthy practice of medicine. Incredibly, and with typical unpredictability, Blood set himself up as a physician about fourteen miles from London in the marketplace at Romford, under the name of Dr Allen or Ayloffe. The idea of him suddenly establishing himself as a doctor in this way may seem strange, but in an era when there was a proliferation of medical quackery it may have been common practice. It was a time when quacks could 'diagnose an illness in the patient's absence, solely from his urine, a practice condemned by the College of Physicians as "piss-pot science"'.[17] Even so-called qualified physicians did not earn their qualifications through study or apprenticeship; they simply bought them.

Despite his haphazard lifestyle during these years Blood did manage to father a number of children. It was with her children William, Holcroft, Edmund, Charles, Mary and Elizabeth that Maria moved into an apothecary's shop under the name of Weston in Shoreditch.[18] Their eldest son, Thomas, now in his late teens, was apprenticed to an apothecary called Samuel Holmes in Southwark.[19] He later left this establishment and set up his own shop. Apothecaries at this time were expected to give a wide range of medical advice and they sold a range of homemade potions over the counter to remedy everything from a cough to loss of virility.

By now the elder Blood, probably feeling that his notoriety had been added to by the Mason escape, was referring to himself not as Captain but as Major Blood.

Even the informer William Leving refers to him as such in a letter in 1667.[20] There is no record of how proficient he was at his new career of medicine or how successful his practice became but, in any event, he did not stay dedicated to his new calling for long.

7

JAMES THE WHITE

James Butler, 1st Duke of Ormonde, came from an eminent family of Anglo-Norman descent.[1] The family name of Butler was derived from the position of Chief Butler of Ireland, which was held by Ormonde's ancestor Theobald Walter, who died in 1206. As the centuries passed the Butler family amassed considerable wealth, property and influence. The first earl, who died in 1338, also had the name James Butler and was married to the granddaughter of Edward II of England.

One of the most memorable Butlers was Thomas Butler, born in 1531. He was only fourteen when his father died along with a steward and sixteen servants when they were poisoned at a banquet. Thomas, who became the 10th Earl of Ormonde, was reared at court and shared a tutor with Edward VI. 'Black Tom', as he was known, went on to enjoy royal favour not only during Edward's reign but also that of Mary and his distant cousin Elizabeth. In fact so close was his acquaintance with that often difficult monarch, Elizabeth I, that he was able to tell her to her face that her favourite, Robert Dudley, the Earl of Leicester, was a 'villain and a coward' and live to tell the tale.[2] At one point he even challenged Leicester to armed combat, a challenge which was not taken up. On another occasion, when Leicester cheekily greeted him with the comment that he had in his dreams given him a box on the ear the night before, Black Tom replied pithily that 'dreams are to be interpreted by contraries' and on the spot gave Leicester an actual box on the ear! On the strength of this encounter the Queen did send her cousin to the Tower for a short time and afterwards insisted on a reconciliation between the two men. It was a reconciliation performed publicly if not entirely sincerely.[3]

Despite having been married three times, Black Tom had only two sons, who both predeceased him. As a result, when he died in 1614 at the age of eighty-three with no living male heir, his titles went to his nephew Walter Butler, who became the 11th Earl of Ormonde. However, Walter's accession was challenged by Lord Dingwall, Richard Preston, who was the second husband of Black Tom's daughter, Elizabeth. Preston was supported in his claim by James I. Walter, rather foolishly it seems, signed a bond in £100,000 to abide by the King's arbitration on the matter, perhaps expecting the King to act impartially. However, James duly awarded 'the Castle of Kilkenny, the House of Dunmore and the better half of the entire estates' to Preston.[4] This of course was to leave Walter in a very awkward position financially and began what was to be one of the most difficult times in the long history of the Butler family. Walter was even imprisoned for contempt of court until he agreed to accept the King's decision.[5]

To add to Walter's troubles, his son and heir, Thomas, was shipwrecked and drowned in 1619. So it came about that the family line of succession passed on to Thomas's son, James Butler, the Ormonde of this story. James had been born to Elizabeth Poyntz, the wife of Thomas Butler, on 19 October 1610 at Clerkenwell. It seems that as a child Ormonde had been a particular favourite of Black Tom's. He is reputed to have once, while stroking the child's head, made the prophetic comment: 'my family shall be much oppressed and brought very low, but by this boy it shall be restored again and in his time be in greater splendour than it has ever been'.[6]

Ormonde was only a boy of around nine at the time of his father's tragic drowning. His mother sent him to be educated at a Roman Catholic school at Finchley. However, so important was the Butler family that King James, on hearing that such a person was receiving a Roman Catholic education, became disturbed and had him sent instead to Lambeth to reside in the palace of the Archbishop of Canterbury. The Archbishop took on the responsibility as requested but seems to have been none too pleased about it, in large part perhaps because he received no payment for his trouble. Although Ormonde lived as a member of the Archbishop's family until he was sixteen, in effect very little care was taken with his education and many gaps in it had to be filled in later on.[7] One effect of that time may have been the devotion to Anglicanism that he was to have for the rest of his life. From the age of sixteen he went to live with his grandfather in Ireland. It is said that during this time he learned to speak enough of the Irish language to be able to hold a conversation in it.[8]

Meanwhile Richard Preston, Earl of Desmond and holder of the Ormonde land, had only one child by his wife Elizabeth. Their young daughter, also named Elizabeth, was now heir to the Ormonde land. It was said that George Villiers, the 1st Duke of Buckingham, had plans to marry his nephew to Elizabeth. Poor Elizabeth's young world was suddenly turned upside down when both of her parents died within a few weeks of one another in 1628. Her father was drowned at sea, while her mother died of natural causes at home. With her dying breath Elizabeth's mother had urged her to marry her cousin, James Butler, and thereby end the split in their family.[9] Now an orphan, at the young age of thirteen Elizabeth was placed in the guardianship of the Earl of Holland.

Although neither the Holland household nor Charles I

was in favour of the match, the first move towards building a relationship between the young Ormonde and Elizabeth Preston was taken when it was arranged by a third party that he should see her at church one Sunday morning. He must have liked what he saw because some time later he arrived at the Holland house disguised as a peddler and the young lovers managed to pass notes secretly.[10]

For some time letter writing between the sweethearts continued alongside political wrangling between their elders, until finally in 1629 the young Ormonde, at this time Lord Thurles, married his cousin Baroness Dingwall, Elizabeth Preston. In one move, she being heiress to the Butler lands and he to the title of Earl of Ormonde, land and title were once again united. The couple lived for a year with Ormonde's uncle in Gloucester and then went to live in Ormonde Castle at Carrick-on-Suir in County Tipperary, Ireland, with his grandfather Walter. From then on Ireland was to play the predominant role in the life of the man the Irish would refer to as 'James the White' on account of his fair complexion.[11]

In 1631 Ormonde purchased a troop in the standing army in Ireland and in 1632, following Walter's death, assumed the prestigious title of 12th Earl of Ormonde. The following year he offered his services to the Lord Deputy of Ireland, Sir Thomas Wentworth. At a meeting of Parliament in July 1634 he was selected to carry the Sword of State before the Lord Deputy. An event that unfolded at a meeting of Parliament in 1634 illustrates clearly the developing determination and confidence of the young Ormonde. Fear of trouble between MPs had made the Lord Deputy order that no one be permitted to enter the chamber while wearing a sword. However, on his arrival at the door Ormonde refused to hand over his sword when requested and, when pressed on the matter by the Usher of the Black Rod whose responsibility it was to ensure that no one entered armed, he firmly informed the man 'that if he had his sword, it should be in his guts'. He then walked resolutely to his seat.[12] He is reputed to have been the only peer to sit in the House that day wearing his sword.

When he heard of this display of arrogance and impudence the Lord Deputy's initial reaction was annoyance. But after giving some thought to the issue and having listened to some advice he seems to have concluded that such a determined character as Ormonde would be better as a friend than an adversary. In any event, it was not long after this incident that at the age of twenty-four Ormonde was made a member of the Privy Council. Promoted to the command of a troop of Cuirassiers in 1638 at around the age of twenty-eight, he was later promoted to the rank of Lieutenant-General and acted as Commander-in-Chief of the forces in the kingdom of Ireland whenever the Earl of Strafford was out of the country.

It comes as no surprise then to discover that when the Roman Catholic rebellion broke out in Ireland in 1641 Ormonde was appointed Commander-in-Chief of the King's army and was to play a major role in that long and violent struggle. On 7 November 1642 he was named Marquis of Ormonde and was appointed Lord Lieutenant of Ireland by Charles I in 1644. Developments in the English Civil War and the fact that the Roman Catholic rebels in Ireland declared their support for the King in opposition to a Puritan Parliament forced Ormonde to put aside his staunch Protestant feelings and negotiate with the rebels. This ultimately led to the two peace treaties of 1646 and 1649.

Meanwhile by 1646 Elizabeth had given birth to eight sons and two daughters. However, the couple had already experienced more than their fair share of sadness, having suffered the deaths of four of their sons. In 1646 yet another horrific tragedy befell them. One day the family nurse decided to take the children out for some air in their father's coach, when the horses took fright and bolted. In her panic the nurse decided that the safest thing to do with the baby boy was to throw him out of the window and free of the coach. Unfortunately, the fall proved fatal.[13]

When in July 1647 Ormonde effectively handed over Dublin and the other towns in his control to the Parliamentary forces, he fled first to England and later to France. By 1648 he was back in Ireland again by royal request, negotiating the treaty of 1649 and finding himself in command of all the Royalist troops in the country. He had survived a shipwreck on his way back to Ireland when he accepted passage on a boat carrying cider. When the master of the boat enquired of Ormonde what time of day it was, Ormonde gave him a time that was wrong by one hour. The mistake seems to have caused the man to miscalculate his position and he ran the ship on to rocks which split it. Ormonde only managed to survive by reaching shallow water in a small boat.[14]

Not only the news, but also the manner of the death of Charles I must have come as a terrible blow to Ormonde, so close had they been throughout many difficult years. However, Ormonde went on stoically with his task of combining the two disparate elements of the Royalist forces and the rebels into one army and gaining military control of much of Ireland. This he managed admirably until the arrival of the military might of Oliver Cromwell. Although the two men never met, Cromwell once described Ormonde rather disparagingly, on seeing a portrait of him, as more like a huntsman than a soldier.[15] It was Cromwell who finally defeated Ormonde's forces and conquered Ireland. Cromwell also assumed Ormonde's title of Lord Lieutenant of Ireland in June 1649.

Ormonde was forced to flee 'Cromwellian' Ireland and go to the exiled Court of the young Charles II on the continent. It cannot have been easy for a man who was so accustomed to controlling political events to find himself in exile and removed from power. It was also a great shock for one used to living in grandeur to find himself forced to live in much simpler conditions. As he had left Ireland with no more than £500, he found himself having to travel the streets on foot and not in the grand carriage he had been used to. He was also forced to rely on the generosity of nobles in France and elsewhere.[16] He spoke of 'the want of money that makes us mad'.[17]

On one occasion, having enjoyed a meal at a nobleman's house in Laye, Ormonde, wishing to give something in return for the hospitality he had received, gave ten pistoles to the servants to share among themselves. It was all the money he had that day. However, on his way home he was amazed to find the nobleman furiously following him up the road, calling after him. Apparently the man had heard his servants arguing about the division of the money. He angrily informed Ormonde that he paid his servants an adequate amount and that he expected them to serve his friends as well as himself. He demanded that Ormonde take the money back or else 'give him the usual satisfaction of men of honour for an avowed affront'.[18] Ormonde accepted the money.

The dire financial situation felt by members of the nobility in this situation is also portrayed in a letter written at the time by Edward Hyde, 1st Earl of Clarendon:

> I am sure the King owes for all he hath eaten since April
> . . . five or six of us eat together one meal a day for a
> pistole a week, but all of us owe for God knows how
> many weeks to the poor woman who feeds us. I believe
> my lord of Ormonde hath not had 5 livres in his purse
> this month and hath fewer clothes . . .[19]

With Ormonde's financial situation as it was, something had to be done. It was 1652, the war was over in Ireland, and Cromwell's regime was in the process of dividing the land up among those who had assisted in the war effort. It was decided that if Lady Ormonde, the Marchioness of Ormonde, was to go to England she might be able to reclaim at least some part of their estate, especially since it had been her own inheritance. If they were to do so this was the opportune time for her to argue the case.

In August 1652 the Marchioness left France and sailed for England. However, things did not run smoothly for her claim. Her case was referred to the Lord Deputy and Council because her lands were within the so-called 'Irish quarters'.[20] Her claim was not helped by the fact that she was a Roman Catholic. It was the beginning of what was to be a struggle for her. In the Marchioness's favour was the fact that Cromwell held her in high esteem and had in fact already declared that her estate should not be given away to anyone.[21] She wrote to him requesting his help.[22] She also had many witnesses willing to testify to her character and to the kind deeds she had done for English soldiers during the war.

Finally, by February of 1653, the Marchioness managed to obtain an Order of Parliament by which the Commissioners for the Affairs of Ireland could set apart Dunmore House near Kilkenny for herself and the children with lands to the value of £2,000 a year as set in the year 1640. All of this was with the proviso that this income was to provide for herself and the children and not for her husband. With the necessary Order in hand she set off for Dublin and by December her case was being dealt with by the Commissioners. However, her troubles were not yet over. The Marchioness soon discovered that the yearly value of the lands being assigned to her would fall far short of that which had been set by Parliament after all charges on it were taken into account. Finally, after much effort on her part, the matter was settled by the granting of extra leases to her.[23] Having at last achieved her goal she set sail for England to fetch the children.

But even then her difficulties did not end. She arrived back in England only to have her son, Thomas, Earl of Ossory, thrown in the Tower by Cromwell on suspicion of plotting against him. When the Marchioness received no satisfaction from writing to Cromwell she went to see the Protector in person to plead her son's case. Once again Cromwell treated her with great respect and was prepared to discuss the matter in a civil manner with her. 'He treated her indeed always with the greatest civility; never refused her an audience; and when she went away, he always waited on her to her coach or chair; a respect which he never paid to any body else.'[24] After some time she managed to have her son released from captivity when he became ill. After a period of being looked after by his mother it was decided that Ossory's illness would best respond to a change in climate, so he left with his brother Richard for Flanders and later Holland, while their mother sailed for Ireland with the other children. Although Ormonde did not see his wife again until after the Restoration, he must have gained considerable peace of mind from the knowledge that she and the children were safe and living in relative comfort.

Ormonde himself secretly visited London in 1657 to assess the degree of support and readiness for a rebellion being planned by Charles with the help of Spain. By all accounts he spent what was a miserable month being chased around the city by Cromwell's men while he wore a wig that changed colour every time it rained![25] In any event the proposed rebellion never took place.

With the death of Cromwell and the eventual restoration of the monarchy in 1660, Ormonde found himself back once again at the centre of power. He was, as it has been put, 'happy in the favour of his prince, and in the esteem of the world, and dignified with various honours and employments'.[26] Charles II made him a sworn member of the Privy Council, Lord Steward of the Household, Lord Lieutenant for the County of Somerset, High Steward of Westminster, Kingston and Bristol. He was created Earl of Brecknock and Baron of Llanthony, and was also restored to his position as Chancellor of the University and College of Dublin. He was given back the lands comprising the

County of Tipperary in Ireland that had been seized from his grandfather by James I. Along with all this, Ormonde's ancient right as hereditary Chief Butler to the prisage of wine was restored to him, a right which entitled him to two tons for every eighteen tons of wine cargo imported into Ireland on which he was exempt from paying excise.

In March 1661 he was raised to the title of 1st Duke of Ormonde in the Irish peerage and created Lord High Steward of England. The fact that Ormonde was an extremely powerful man of position and wealth is attested to by the fact that at Charles II's coronation he marched 'in the solemn procession immediately before his majesty, and carrying in his hands St. Edward's crown'.[27]

Appointed Lord Lieutenant of Ireland after General Monck, Ormonde made his return to Dublin as part of an impressive procession, travelling the last two miles not in his coach but on horseback. The occasion was marked by the attendance of large crowds entertained with music, bonfires and fireworks. He received a gold bowl from the Lord Mayor valued at £400 and the freedom of the city.[28] He took up residence at the Phoenix Lodge.

However, it was not long until Protestant discontent over the way the land question was being handled by the Court of Claims led to Blood's plot of 1663, wherein an attempt was to be made to capture Dublin Castle and Ormonde himself. The plot has been described as

a dramatic reflection of the deeply held conviction which existed among the Protestants that the commissioners of the Court of Claims were intent on dismantling the entire settlement and that this process must be reversed and the Act of Settlement amended, in order to protect the existing proprietors.[29]

Although Blood's plot did not go ahead it had the desired effect of forcing the authorities into reviewing their handling of the land question. After much negotiation between the opposing parties, and much effort on the part of Ormonde, the Act of Explanation passed through the Irish Parliament in 1665. Although the Act very clearly favoured Protestants and caused much discontent among Roman Catholics, it effectively brought the issue of land settlement in Ireland to a conclusion.

By now it was the late 1660s and a number of conditions were conspiring to make Ormonde's position as Lord Lieutenant of Ireland precarious.[30] Firstly, the Chancellor, Clarendon, had been impeached and driven from office in 1667 and Ormonde's own position had relied to a great extent on the Chancellor's support. The new administration, known as the CABAL, was also hostile to Ormonde. To make matters worse, Barbara Villiers, the King's formidable mistress, bore Ormonde a personal grudge. She had set her heart on owning the Phoenix Park and House near Dublin and had managed to obtain a warrant for the grant of the same from the King. But Ormonde had other plans for the place. Since Dublin Castle was in poor repair he wanted to enlarge the park and use the house as a residence for himself and his successors. Consequently, when it came before him, he refused to pass Barbara's warrant and instead pushed ahead to fulfil his own plans. This enraged Barbara and when she next came upon Ormonde at court in England 'she fell upon him with a torrent of abusive language . . . and told him . . . that she hoped to see him hanged'.[31] He is reputed to have replied calmly that 'he was not in so much haste to put an end to her days, for all he wished with regard to her was, that he might live to see her old'.[32]

Added to all this there was bad feeling between Ormonde and the Queen Mother, Henrietta-Maria, which came about mainly as a result of disputes between the two regarding the restoration to their estates of various dispossessed Roman Catholics whom the Queen Mother wished to see restored. In one famous case, she wanted the Marquis of Antrim restored and Ormonde refused to comply.

Possibly the most significant of Ormonde's enemies at the time was George Villiers, the 2nd Duke of Buckingham, and Barbara's cousin. Growing tensions led to a public row in 1666 between Buckingham and Ormonde's son, the Earl of Ossory. Buckingham was a firm supporter of the proposed law that would impose limits on the import of Irish cattle into England. This being a time when Ireland needed every financial support it could get, Ormonde and his sons opposed the Bill vehemently. During the debate on the Irish Cattle Bill in the House of Lords Buckingham made the remark that no one was against the Bill except those who had either Irish estates or Irish understandings. Ossory took exception to this comment and insisted that Buckingham meet him at Chelsea Fields at a time agreed between them wherein he would get satisfaction. At the appointed time Ossory arrived and waited in vain for three hours for Buckingham. Instead of keeping the appointment, however, Buckingham ran to the King and informed him of the incident. The only people to arrive at Chelsea Fields were the guards with a royal warrant to arrest Ossory, who was held for a time but eventually released.

The following morning Buckingham made a speech to the House of Commons informing the members of Ossory's challenge to him. He told the members that he had waited for Ossory to arrive at the agreed place until he was ordered to leave by a gentleman who had been sent by the King. Ossory for his part informed the House that his challenge was issued not directly because of comments made in the House but because he had for some time grown weary of Buckingham's many insults. Both men were required to withdraw from the House while the event was examined. In the end a rebuke for both parties followed by a short stay in the Tower was deemed to be a sufficient punishment.[33]

However, by the late 1660s Buckingham was enjoying considerable influence with the King and he was one of the main instigators of the removal from office of Clarendon on 30 August 1667. There is no doubt that Buckingham next set his sights upon the removal of Ormonde from the Lord Lieutenancy of Ireland. In fact he had designs on the titles of Lord Lieutenant of Ireland and Steward of the Household for himself.

Buckingham faced two major obstacles to the removal of Ormonde. First, the undoubted high esteem in which Ormonde was generally held; second, the fact that he had committed no wrong that Buckingham and his friends could use against him.[34] Nevertheless in October 1667 Buckingham, assisted by Sir Robert Howard, came up with twelve articles of impeachment against Ormonde. Howard's motivation was the grudge he held against the Duke for his failure to be appointed as a Commissioner for administering the Act of Explanation.

For Ormonde's part he felt that he could not be accused by 'more inconsiderable fellows or more detested knaves'.[35] However, Buckingham also managed to enlist the assistance of a one-time friend of Ormonde's, Roger Boyle, the Earl of Orrery, in this attack. Orrery's accusations were of financial impropriety in the administration of Ireland. Buckingham managed to persuade Parliament to appoint a committee, of which he was a member, to examine the Duke's administration of Ireland. Ormonde took this development seriously enough to travel to England in 1668, leaving his son Ossory in his place. On his arrival in England Buckingham even had the audacity to pay him a ceremonial visit, assuring the Duke that he wished him no harm.[36]

One day in 1669 Ormonde was told by his chaplain, Dr Sheridan, that at a party the previous evening Buckingham and his supporters had at last persuaded the King to remove him from the Lord Lieutenancy of Ireland.[37] The accuracy of this report was soon proved to Ormonde when this was exactly what occurred. It was, however, a course of action that the King seemed to regret.

'His majesty on this occasion declared, how well he was satisfied with the duke of Ormond's thirty years' service to his father and himself'.[38] In addition, events did not work out exactly in the Duke of Buckingham's favour, because, as Carte puts it, the King resolved 'not to give the post to any of those who had openly aimed at it, and had shewed themselves most active and busy in attacking the Duke of Ormond'.[39] Instead the unpopular Lord Robartes was appointed as new Lord Lieutenant of Ireland, a man described as 'morose, overbearing, and impracticable'.[40] This appointment angered Buckingham, who had already begun to offer posts as gifts to people in expectation of gaining the appointment. Robartes's appointment was short-lived and some seven months later Lord Berkeley of Stratton replaced him.

In the meantime Ormonde was unanimously elected Chancellor of the University of Oxford on 26 August 1669. Buckingham's vendetta against the Duke was not over yet, as he persevered with trying to have him removed from the Stewardship of the Household by attacking him whenever he could. On this issue the King failed to be moved.

It was at this rather low point in his life that Ormonde was about to come face to face with another adversary.

8

AN AUDACIOUS KIDNAPPING

It was in 1670, three years after the rescue of Captain Mason, that Thomas Blood was to reappear from hiding, abandon his medical career and embark on another daring and audacious deed. In that year he left Romford and we find him moving to Aldgate, near the Tower of London. On Tuesday 6 December a grand feast was being held at the Guildhall in honour of the Prince of Orange, who was on his first official visit to England. His uncle, Charles II, had a secret agreement in place with the French at the time and his political aim may have been to evaluate where William might stand on any such matter.[1] On this particular night the King had organised a major social event to honour his nephew, with all the important aristocrats of the time in attendance.

The Lord High Steward of His Majesty's Household and former Lord Lieutenant of Ireland, the Duke of Ormonde, was one of those enjoying the festivities that night. The Duke was not a young man any more and on the winter's night in question he decided to leave the festivities early. He was staying at the time in Clarendon House, which had been lent him by the former Chancellor's son. This fine house was at the upper end of the street leading from St James's Palace. In keeping with his substantial wealth and standing in society, it was the

Duke's habit to travel in a great coach attended by an entourage. His coach was instantly recognisable from the spikes fixed to its side to prevent the footmen or torchbearers from climbing on, thereby forcing them to walk or run instead.

Matthew Pretty and a boy called William Wilson worked at the Bull Head tavern in Charing Cross. Between six and seven o'clock on the evening in question they remembered five men entering the premises.[2] The Bull Head was a favourite hostelry, where people like Samuel Pepys often spent an enjoyable evening. Of one such occasion Pepys wrote: 'we dined at the Bullhead upon the best venison pasty that ever I eat of in my life, and with one dish more it was the best dinner that I ever was at'.[3]

Pretty and Wilson stated that they did not know the five men who arrived that evening on horses and carrying swords. The men ordered six pints of wine, two pints each of 'canary, sherry and white wine'.[4] One of them made a point of telling the drawer to draw good wine for them as they were graziers. When the drawer asked them if they knew two graziers called West and Pountney, they said they did. The drawer described two of them as young men about twenty-six years of age, and the other three as middle-aged. One of them, 'a tall, lean, pale-faced man, with short black hair', rode upon 'a reddish dark horse with a bald face'.[5] But the drawer believed that the man was wearing a wig.

At around seven o'clock both witnesses heard the shout 'Make way here for the Duke of Ormonde!', which came from out on the street, and afterwards they saw the Duke's coach pass by. Shortly after this the men paid their wine bill, purchased three pipes of tobacco and were seen riding off at 'a good pace' towards the Hay Market or Pall Mall. The boy Wilson duly drank their unfinished wine!

No one imagined that as powerful a figure as the Duke of Ormonde was in danger of being attacked in London that night. But the determined intention of Thomas Blood and his accomplices, as they left the Bull Head tavern in haste that evening, was to mount such an attack. At the top of St James's Street the Duke's coachman, Henley, was confronted by the sight of a man on horseback shouting at him to stop the coach because there was a dead man lying on the roadway in front of him. As the man brought the Duke's coach to a halt he found himself surrounded by Blood and his men, the horses were seized and the footman, Exby, who was at the back of the coach, had two pistols put to his chest.

With that, Ormonde was ordered to step down. He replied from inside the coach that if it was money they were after, they could have it. Then he found himself being pulled from his coach unceremoniously and forced up on to a horse behind one of the gang members. Ormonde was then promptly tied to the man on the horse and they rode off behind the others down Piccadilly.

The determined Ormonde was not ready to give up so easily. As they rode along, Blood having gone on ahead, some say to prepare the rope for the Duke's hanging, Ormonde began to struggle wildly. Although sixty years of age at the time, he managed to get his foot under his captor's and dismount them both. Once on the ground and rolling in the mud and darkness of the London street he grabbed the man's sword and wriggled free from his binding. By this time some of Ormonde's staff, who had been fetched by the coachman, came running to his aid.

Thomas Brooks, the porter at Clarendon House, was one of those who came to rescue the Duke. As he arrived on the scene Brooks heard the attackers shout 'Kill the rogue'. Two shots rang out as, in a final desperate attempt to carry out their mission, Blood's men fired at the Duke of Ormonde. The Duke was saved only by the darkness of the evening, which caused them to miss. The Duke's assailants had no option now but to retreat without their prisoner. They made their getaway to

Fulham Ferry, where they crossed the Thames and carried on through Lambeth and Southwark. After this their trail was lost, although three horses were discovered, one of which was described as 'a chestnut mare with a blaze down the face'.[6] Although Ormonde was left dirty and shaken from the attack, and had to stay in bed for some days afterwards, his wounds were not serious and he managed to make a full recovery.

We cannot be sure what Blood and his men had intended to do with Ormonde that evening. Some said that they were planning to hold him to ransom for the return of Blood's land in Ireland, while others proposed that it had been their sole intention to bring the Duke to Tyburn and hang him there like a common criminal at the place of public execution.[7] Whatever Blood's intentions were, the establishment figures of the time were in uproar at the audacity of such an attack, none more so than the King himself, who was furious. He issued a Proclamation dated 7 December 1670:

Whereas upon Tuesday, the sixth of this instant December, between the hours of six and seven in the evening, a barbarous and inhumane attempt was made upon the person and life of our right trusty, and right entirely beloved cousin and counsellor James Duke of Ormond, who was set upon in the street as he was going in his coach, between St. James and Clarendon house, by six persons armed and mounted on horses, who forced him out of his coach, and then caused him to be set on horseback, behind one of their company, with intent to have carried him to some obscure place out of town, where they might with more privacy have executed their villainous and bloody conspiracy, until at last, the said Duke endeavouring to rescue himself, by disarming and dismounting him that rode before him, was very much wounded in that conflict, and now lies languishing under those wounds, at his lodgings in Clarendon

House; The bold assassinates having made shift to escape all pursuit by reason of the darkness of the night: We have thought fit by this our Royal Proclamation, to publish and declare, that whosoever shall discover unto us, or any of our privy council, or any other of our magistrates or officers, any one of these six persons, or any of their aidors, or abettors, and shall cause him to be arrested and seized upon, he shall, for such his pains and diligence in this affair, receive from us a reward of one thousand pounds sterling; and moreover, shall be further esteemed and considered by us, as one who hath done us, a most eminent and most acceptable service.[8]

The *London Gazette* the following Thursday carried a report on the attack with information regarding the substantial reward of £1,000 and a description of one of the suspects' horses.[9] Everywhere in taverns and coffee-houses this daring attack was discussed in detail, with some even claiming that the intention of those blaggards had been to sell the Duke into slavery with the Moors![10] The ports were watched, the local authorities put on the look-out and all available informers put to work. These culprits had to be identified and hunted down.

A preliminary investigation was conducted by the Lord Mayor, Sir Richard Ford, and Mr Justice Hooker, while Lord Arlington began examining witnesses.[11] Intelligence was sought from many sources and much began to come in, such as the following, which is taken from an unsigned letter:

I am told that Allin or Ayliffe, mentioned in the *Gazette*, as one of the persons suspected in the attempt on the Duke of Ormonde, was at sea in the Portland frigate, and that Jennings or Jennins, who was formally surgeon to that ship, is a great crony of his and a likely man to give an account of him. Jennings lives over against the Coach and Horses, in St. Martin's Lane, and his wife works at the Exchange; it will not be amiss to call upon him when you go that way . . .[12]

The following letter written by Sir William Morton, Justice of the King's Bench, to Under-Secretary Williamson regarding information coming from his informants shows how the regime's contacts were put to work in an effort to track down those who were guilty:

I asked Washwhite whether he when in Ireland knew Moore or Blood, and, as I remember, he told me he had heard of such men, but did not know them, but would inquire after them. I told him, if he would find them out in town and bring me word of them I would gratify him for his pains; he said he would endeavour it. I employed Sebastian Jones on the discovery of Moore and Blood, who knew them in Ireland, who told me he knew some acquaintances of theirs here, and since has told me that Blood lives in Lancashire, but he cannot yet hear of Moore. He gives me some hope of discovering something of the Duke of Ormonde's business, and is to give me an account in two days.[13]

A House of Lords Committee of sixty-nine was established in January 1671 to examine the evidence and subsequently a sub-committee also looked into the crime. Eventually the three prime suspects were identified as Dr Thomas Allen (or Ayloffe, Aylett, Alec), Mr Thomas Hunt and Mr Richard Halliwell (or Holloway), who were described as 'Fifth Monarchy men and desperate'.[14]

Lord Arlington had intelligence dating from the 1660s that the name Allen was an alias often used by Thomas Blood.[15] The first evidence to link the name 'Dr Allen' with this attack on the Duke was some letters from him that were found in the lodgings of both Hunt and Halliwell. Then one Michael Beresford, a clergyman, stated that he had held a conversation with this man, whom he knew as

Dr Allen, in the Piazza, Covent Garden, at six o'clock that evening, which placed the suspect in the vicinity of the crime. He described him as a 'very fine man, with a brown perriwig' and said that he had lately come from Ireland.[16] A man called Bloxton, a tailor, stated that he knew the suspect as Dr Alec but that he was aware that the man also wrote his name as Allen, Eylett, or Ayloffe. He had recently asked Bloxton to act as one of the sureties for a Thomas Hunt, who had been arrested.

The fact that the man calling himself 'Thomas Hunt' was actually Blood's eldest son Thomas was also soon discovered by the investigators. Thomas Blood junior had lately taken to the practice of highway robbery and Hunt was an alias he used while engaged in that activity. They also knew that although the suspect had lived in Ireland he had not been born there. He was described by witnesses who knew him as a 'young, tall, ruddy man' and a 'lusty, proper young man, full faced, about 21 years of age'.[17] At the scene of the struggle between the man on horseback and Ormonde, a sword, belt and pistol were found on the ground. One vital piece of evidence was the pistol, which was of the small 'pocket screwed' variety, garnished with silver and marked with the initials 'T.H.'.[18] As it happened these same items, including the pistol, had been taken from Thomas Hunt some months previously when he had been arrested at Lambeth on a charge of assaulting and attempting to rob one John Constable.[19] Hunt had been convicted of the crime in July 1670 at Guildford before Chief Justice Keeling and Judge Morton, and was fined 100 marks and imprisoned in the Marshalsea. He was released in August on the strength of two sureties given for his good behaviour for seven years. One of these sureties was provided by a brewer named Mumford, who now stated that he had been 'drawn into it', and the other by Bloxton, who was asked to do so by the man he knew as Dr Alec. Hunt's property was returned to him in October. The receipt made out on their return to him was witnessed by one Edmond Hunt.[20] This was probably Thomas's brother, Edmund Blood. The weapons and belt found at the scene of the attack on the Duke of Ormonde were positively identified as being the same by a constable named Thomas Drayton and a man called Henry Partridge.[21]

The investigators discovered that Hunt had been lately apprenticed to Holmes the apothecary, who had premises in Southwark. They also knew that after six months he had left Holmes and set up his own enterprise as either an apothecary, a grocer or a mercer depending on the accounts of various witnesses. In his evidence Holmes said that Hunt was a Presbyterian. He was, according to Holmes's servant, at first 'very poor in clothes' and then later 'very fine'.[22] This, one assumes, was a result of his increased income as a highwayman.

Twelve-year-old Margaret Boulter, the niece of Richard Halliwell, who was another suspect in this crime, testified that she often saw Hunt at her uncle's house. She said that he was 'a tall, slender, black man, wearing a flaxen perruque', but rather confusingly she states that he often went by the name of 'Dr Allen'.[23] In further damning evidence against him eyewitnesses actually placed Hunt in the vicinity of the crime on the evening of the attack. On 9 January Sir Robert Vyner had Hunt's lodgings searched.

Richard Halliwell, a tobacco cutter from Frying Pan Alley, Petticoat Lane, Bishopsgate Street, London, was the other main suspect in this crime.[24] Halliwell (or Hollowell, Holloway), known as a Fifth Monarchy man, had formerly been a cornet in the army. He had a reputation for militant support of Protestant non-conformity. He only just managed to escape out of a garret window when the Lord Mayor and Sir Robert Vyner turned up at his lodgings at two o'clock on the morning of 10 December to question him. Their visit was not in vain, however, as they found three incriminating letters there, two of which were from the suspect known as Dr Allen and the other written by Halliwell himself. The letter by Halliwell, entitled his 'Letter to the Church', in which he declared his religious views, contained material that, according to the Committee of investigation, was 'full of traitorous matter and shows him to be a dangerous person'.[25] In one of his letters Dr Allen had requested the loan of some pistols. A wet cloak discovered at the lodgings also raised suspicions. When Halliwell's wife Katherine was questioned she said she knew nothing of the affair but did admit that it was she who had brought that cloak to him. His niece, Margaret Boulter, stated that Halliwell had been at home on the night of the attack from around eight or nine o'clock.

Although in hiding, Halliwell sent a letter to the Lord Mayor claiming that he was not involved in the attack on the Duke of Ormonde, and explaining that he had run away only because of the severity of treatment being received by those who had already been arrested on suspicion of this crime.[26] He complained about the arrest of his wife and child, and explained that Dr Allen's letter about the pistols was an old one left inadvertently in a coat pocket since the previous spring. He claimed that the doctor had only needed the weapons for an adventure at sea. That wet cloak, he claimed, had nothing to do with him. Mrs Somes, who was Halliwell's aunt, provided an alibi for him on the evening of the attack.

The investigation also revealed that at the time of the attack on the Duke, Blood's wife Maria was found to have left the apothecary's in Shoreditch, where she had been living with her children, and had moved to the house of a schoolmaster called Jonathan Daveys at Mortlake. However, in his evidence Mr Daveys stated that she had disappeared from his house on the morning of the attack on the Duke of Ormonde.[27]

When they searched Mr Daveys's house the investigators found a letter signed 'T.A.' and addressed to Mrs Mary Hunt, dated 17 November 1670. They had a strong suspicion that those initials suggested that it had been written by Thomas Allen, i.e. Blood himself. The letter includes the following, which suggests the organisation of some future event: 'I would have Thomas to come unto mee to my lodging on Fryday morning; let him bring his cloake with him, wee thinke about the begining of the weeke if God give an oportunity to sign the agreement, which is all at present from Your friend, T.A.'[28]

The Thomas referred to here could well be Thomas Blood junior. But what agreement is he waiting for the opportunity to sign and with whom? Is this agreement with the person who was really behind the attack on the Duke of Ormonde? Was that agreement with Ormonde's enemy, the Duke of Buckingham?

Apart from the main suspects, the names of those thought to have played at least some part in the attack included Samuel Holmes, John Hurst, a cook called John Washwhite, a butcher from near Southwark named Thomas Dixey, a well-known radical called William More and a Fifth Monarchist called William Smith.

Holmes was the apothecary and former army surgeon from Scotland to whom Thomas Blood junior had been apprenticed. He was brought before the Lord Mayor and Mr Justice Hooker on 9 December and Lord Arlington on the 12th. He was found to have been in correspondence with the chief suspects in the case. He gave information on Hunt and told them that he also knew a Dr Aylett or Eylott, who was a Presbyterian like Hunt. He had not, he stated, seen either of them for six months. He told them he knew nothing of Hunt's father and that he had never heard of Blood. They failed to find anything on which to prosecute Holmes and he was discharged from custody in January, having given his security to appear before them again if required.[29]

Margaret Boulter had testified to seeing a man called John Hurst, 'of middle stature and no employment', at the house of her uncle Richard Halliwell many times during the two years she had lived there.[30] As the investigators attempted to round up this suspect it resulted in some confusion. Not one, but three men of that name were brought before them.[31] The first was the son of a minister born at Cambridge who had lodged both at the Fleece in Tothill Street and with one John Jones, the Master of the White Swan in Queen Street, Drury Lane. Since he had been arrested in January for a small debt and was already in custody, he was brought from the Marshalsea to appear before the investigating committee. This Hurst was a small, reddish-haired man and turned out not to have been the one seen at Halliwell's house.

The second Hurst seems to have been middle-sized, with yellow hair and only one ear, having lost the other while held in the pillory. He was described by one witness as being 'a great cheat'.[32] He was from Yorkshire and was a lawyer by profession. The evidence states that he had deserted his wife of seven years and, having been lately both in Ireland and Scotland, he now intended to marry a widow at Deptford. Obviously his wife had not seen him for some time, as in her evidence she stated that she did not know whether he had both his ears or not.[33] One witness stated that he had seen him with Halliwell at the Exchange.[34]

By contrast the third Hurst was a mariner from Sussex who had been happily married for only four months. This man was by far the least likely candidate for the crime. He was able to prove his respectability and had a credible alibi for the evening in question. He was with a Captain Lawrence on the night of the attack and Lady Lawrence was willing to vouch for him, having known him fourteen or fifteen years. In the end no solid evidence was found against any of the Hursts and all were freed.

It was the cook, John Washwhite, an informant of Sir William Morton's, who had arrested the first John Hurst. But he too came under suspicion when three witnesses accused him of speaking against the Duke of Ormonde. He was reputed to have said that the Duke would not die in his bed.[35] Consequently Washwhite was arrested and examined before the Committee. He proclaimed his innocence and said that he did not even know Hunt. In fact he stated that he had known nothing at all of the crime until he had arrested Hurst. He once had an address at Lazy Hill, near Dublin, but for the last two years had been living in London. A quarrel he had had with one of the witnesses about a wig and the fact that they were associates of someone he had arrested seem to have been the motivations for these accusations![36] In any event, having heard his statement the Committee thought fit to free him, and he was put back to work gathering information on their behalf.

Thomas Dixey, the butcher from near Southwark, was also reported to have spoken against the Duke of Ormonde. Judge Morton found him to be bold and impudent and was very suspicious of his involvement in the crime. He proved the Judge correct as to his boldness and impudence by his comments on being arrested: 'All they can say is that I said the Duke of Ormonde was a Knave, and I will justify it. I think I shall be hanged, but I care not.'[37] However, when he was examined before the Committee in February he denied the accusation. Dixey's words seem to have consisted more of bravado than anything of substance, since having examined him, the Committee decided to release him on a promise of good behaviour.

Two other characters under suspicion were Humes and More, and evidence was gathered regarding them.[38] Humes was of interest mainly because, according to informers, he was acquainted with Hunt and lodged with Samuel Holmes. They were interested in More because he once owned that infamous pistol of Thomas Hunt's and because he lodged in Gray's Inn Lane, which was a known hiding place of the suspects.

The Duke of Ormonde himself gave evidence on 17

December, although unfortunately his statement is not preserved in the minutes. His coachman Henley, his footman Exby and his porter Brooks all gave evidence as well. Arlington read the following, which was information given to him, to the Committee on 1 February, in which he refers to the fact that the suspects were all religious extremists, although he expressed the belief that most Nonconformists did not support this attack on Ormonde. The piece also reveals his fear that publishing the conspirators' names would only drive them further underground:

> He conceives them all to be desperate men, who shelter themselves under the notion of Fifth Monarchy men. Offers to consideration whether the exposing their names thus by an Act of Parliament will not make them hide themselves with more care, as they do now in the country.[39]

In all, over fifty witnesses were questioned during the investigation and a wealth of documents examined but in the end no sufficient evidence was found to prosecute any of the minor figures. The Committee reported on 17 February and subsequently a bill was drawn up against just three men: Allen (i.e. Blood), Hunt (i.e. Blood junior) and Halliwell. A certain amount of time was allowed for the suspects to surrender themselves voluntarily. Of course they never did and all efforts to have them arrested failed.

While the investigation into the Ormonde kidnapping was going ahead, the authorities were hearing Blood's name associated with yet another dastardly plot.[40] A Richard Wilkinson was telling them that he had heard of a rebel, whom he later found out to be John Mason, who had fifty men ready to attack the gates of Whitehall. This plot, had it gone ahead, would in fact have pre-dated the attack on Ormonde. Wilkinson and other informers named the likes of Blood, Lockyer and Butler as being involved. It would be surprising if Mason were planning something like this for Blood not to be in the middle of it.

Meanwhile Blood, no doubt enjoying his ever-increasing fame, decided to 'promote' himself once again, this time to the rank of Colonel. However, unknown to the authorities, Colonel Blood's most daring deed was yet to come.

9

A COMRADE IN CRIME

Soon after the infamous attack on the Duke of Ormonde another man's name began to be mentioned as the chief instigator of the crime. George Villiers, the 2nd Duke of Buckingham, was one of those who had pushed for the removal of Ormonde from his position as Lord Lieutenant of Ireland and his hatred for the Duke was well known. There is no doubt that at the time of Blood's attack on Ormonde Buckingham would have liked the Duke removed from the political scene altogether. In addition, Buckingham had already shown himself capable of being involved in such criminal activities. It is quite possible that Buckingham employed Blood to murder the Duke. It is impossible to deal with the life of Blood without looking at the life of this equally devious but much more powerful aristocratic rogue.

Apart from his political ambitions Buckingham was an adventurer and writer, and throughout his life was never far from criminality and scandal.[1] He was notorious both politically and sexually and is said to have been 'of all the bad men in a bad time . . . perhaps the worst, without shame, honour, or decency'.[2] His reputation was so bad that he felt the need to write a defence of his character in which he denied that he was a poisoner or had ever practised sodomy.[3]

It is true that a daring kidnap of a duke in the centre of London on an auspicious night is something that would have appealed to Buckingham. As one biographer of his has put it, he

. . . would probably not have considered it ungentlemanlike to slit a rival's throat, by deputy, at a dark corner, but he would have thought it deplorably dull. Whereas, to seize an opponent in the heart of the capital, and in the plenitude of his security, to whirl him to Tyburn, and there, on the gallows to terminate the impeccable career of the Cavalier *sans peur et sans reproche*, was a method of settling accounts, presenting that nice composition of drama and irony dear to the perverted ingenuity of George Villiers.[4]

Born on 30 January 1628, Buckingham's high status in society was clearly shown at his christening ceremony, where none other than Bishop Laud officiated and his godfather was Charles I. His father, the 1st Duke of Buckingham, although without an aristocratic background, had become a man of considerable influence, being the first non-royal duke to be created in over a century. His progress in rank was due to his closeness to James I: the rumour that this was a passionate homosexual relationship had damaged the King's reputation.[5]

After James's death the 1st Duke of Buckingham also became a favourite of Charles I. The Duke's preferential position, along with his unorthodox elevation to the dukedom, meant that he had many enemies and he was assassinated shortly after his son's birth by an army officer called John Felton. Charles I immediately promised the Duchess that 'he would be a father to her children, and a husband to herself'.[6] A few months after her husband's death the Duchess gave birth to another baby boy and thus Buckingham now had a new brother, Francis, and an older sister, Mary.

A few months after Francis's birth the Duchess took the monumental step of reverting to Roman Catholicism, the religion of her birth. Although it must have been a difficult decision for her, in truth her conversion to Protestantism had only ever been for the purpose of marriage to the late Duke. At the same time she also discharged most of the late Duke's Protestant servants.[7] Unfortunately, however, the repercussions of the Duchess's actions were to be felt by her family in a most significant way when the staunchly Protestant King, infuriated by her decision, had the children taken from her. Buckingham and his brother Lord Francis were brought to be raised at court with the Prince of Wales and the Duke of York under the direct guidance of the King himself, while their sister Lady Mary was sent to live with the Pembroke family.[8]

On Christmas Day 1634 Mary, then only twelve years of age, was married to the seventeen-year-old Lord Herbert. After the wedding Lord Herbert was sent to the continent to complete his studies and there he contracted smallpox and died.[9] After this tragedy the young widow was sent to live at court alongside her brothers.

In 1635, when Buckingham's mother decided to marry again, she worsened her reputation with the court of Charles I by marrying the Earl of Antrim, Randal McDonnell, known as 'a fanatical Papist'.[10] This had the effect of hardening the King's attitude even more as regards her contact with the children. In 1636 young Mary was married for the second time, on this occasion to the Duke of Lennox and Richmond, who was a close relative of the King.

At a young age Buckingham and his brother Francis were sent to Trinity College, Cambridge. With the outbreak of the Civil War they went to fight on the side of the King. When Charles heard of their involvement he had them removed from the fighting and sent abroad. They later spent some time at Christ Church, Oxford, continuing their education when a lull in the fighting allowed it. With the

King held as a prisoner on the Isle of Wight and the
Royalist cause looking lost in 1648, Buckingham and his
brother once again entered the fray by fighting with Lord
Holland at Reigate. Unfortunately, Lord Francis was to die
during this battle at the age of twenty. On his dead body
was found a lock of hair belonging to a Mrs Kirke, 'sewed
in a ribbon' next to his heart.[11]

For his part, Buckingham only just managed to escape
capture shortly after the battle by fighting his way out of his
surrounded lodgings. For him capture would have meant
certain death, just as it had for his commander Lord
Holland, who was captured and beheaded. Shortly
afterwards Parliament offered 'liberal terms' to Buckingham
in return for his submission to their authority.[12] However,
his decision to remain loyal to the King cost him all of the
Villiers property and forced him into exile with his childhood
companion the Prince of Wales.

While in exile and deprived of any income, Buckingham
managed to survive for a while by selling off the family's
fine art treasures, which had been smuggled out of
England. For example he sold *Ecce Homo* by Titian to
Archduke Leopold of Prague for over £5,000.[13] However,
the young man's tastes were expensive and maintaining his
lifestyle in exile was going to be no easy matter. He even
decided to employ an alchemist and begin a search for the
philosopher's stone. His enthusiasm for the endeavour was
shared by his friend Prince Charles, and the two young men
were said to have spent many hours together 'over the
retort and crucible'.[14] It has also been claimed that
Buckingham introduced the young royal to many vices
during the time they spent together in Europe.[15]

Buckingham did not spend all of his time in exile,
however. It seems that he could not resist the challenge of
visiting his homeland in disguise on a number of
occasions. Once he even paid for his visit by putting on a
show for large audiences in which he played a fool and
performed ballads. His artistic talents were undeniable.

On another occasion his sister Mary, the Duchess of Richmond, owing to the political situation found herself in prison and was being transferred from Whitehall to Windsor. Without warning the Duchess and her escort were brought to a halt on the road by an insistent jester who wished to entertain them. Mary had no option but to listen to the show, which consisted mostly of material offensive to her, much to the amusement of her guards. When the joker had finished his hilarious show he announced that he wished to present the Duchess with copies of the satirical songs he had sung. This, adding to her embarrassment as it did, was assented to by her guards. As the joker came close to the coach to hand her the papers, Mary was much surprised as he lifted his mask briefly to reveal a familiar face. It was her exiled brother who handed her the bundle of papers containing secret letters before making a theatrical exit.[16]

By 1649 and with Cromwell's defeat of Ireland making any return of the King look very remote indeed, and with his store of art treasures running very low, Buckingham began to think of making a deal with Parliament. He decided to enlist the help of a relative, Lord Basil Feilding, an influential Parliamentarian. He also asked Basil's mother to use her influence with her son on his behalf. However, in a letter to his mother written in July 1649 Lord Basil told her how difficult it would be to get any concessions on Buckingham's behalf, as 'the streame runs soe high against him that the issue is much to be doubted '.[17]

In September 1649, with his father now dead, the young Charles bestowed the Order of the Garter on Buckingham and in April 1650 made him a member of the Privy Council. The Scottish Covenanters proclaimed Charles II their King on the death of his father, and when the Duke of Argyll, the Presbyterian leader in Scotland, made advances towards Charles, Buckingham was one of those who advised him to treat with them. In 1650 the negotiations began at Breda. When Argyll invited Charles to travel to Scotland, Buckingham accompanied the King. As it happened, around this time Buckingham was offered a favourable deal by Parliament to return to his estates, which he now decided to decline.

Although Charles was crowned and a Parliament called in Scotland, it all came to nothing when he marched an army south and was routed by Cromwell. After this, Buckingham was forced to flee to Holland. He is reputed to have made the rather disloyal statement that Charles 'had ill-behaved himself in the battle, and that he lay now hidden in some gentleman's house, and was happier in his own opinion, than if he was upon the throne'.[18]

In retaliation, the Princess of Orange, Mary Stuart, banned Buckingham from her Court. Such was his personality, however, that it was not long before the Duke's inimitable presence was felt at Mary's court again and it was even rumoured that he was making romantic overtures towards the widow. When they became aware of his behaviour, both Charles and the Queen Mother, Henrietta-Maria, were outraged. According to Clarendon, Henrietta's opinions on the romance were very clear: 'that if it were possible for her daughter to entertain so base a thought, she would tear her in pieces with her own hands'.[19] From this extreme reaction it is reasonable to assume that there was a mutual attraction at play here, although in the end Buckingham was firmly rejected by the Princess.

Buckingham was angered not only by this rebuttal of his affections but also by the fact that he had not been paid by Charles for a number of years. His thoughts soon turned once again to making a deal with Parliament and returning home. This time he turned to one John Lilburne for assistance. Lilburne may not have been the best choice as an intermediary since he was having problems of his own with the authorities in England. His public opposition to Cromwell, who had once been his idol, led to his banishment in 1651. When he returned to England in June 1653 he was arrested. In fact one of the accusations thrown at him at the time was his close association with the Duke of Buckingham. During the trial he spoke freely of his acquaintance with the Duke, stating that: 'if ever it should lye in my power to do him any personal service, without detriment to my native country (which I am confident he would never desire of me) I judge myself bound in conscience and gratitude to travel on his errand a thousand and a thousand miles upon my feet'.[20]

As the jury had thrown out the charges against Lilburne, Buckingham thought this an opportune time to return home. It was said, by Clarendon among others, that Buckingham's ambitious plan was to marry Cromwell's daughter in order to ensure the return of his lands.[21] However, the reception received by Buckingham was far from friendly and he was soon forced to flee England once again.

Joining the French army as a volunteer, he became involved in fighting against Spain. While he was occupied with this, his enemies at court, chief among them Clarendon, were busy blackening his name with Charles. They related his approaches to the Cromwellian regime and his designs on Cromwell's daughter. They even claimed that he was informing on their activities to Cromwell.[22] The suspicions raised by these accusations understandably led to Buckingham being kept on the outside of Charles's close circle.

In 1657 a relative of Buckingham's, Lord Fairfax, was granted a large part of the Villiers property, to the value of around £5,000 a year.[23] It did not take very long for the Duke to arrive on Lord Fairfax's doorstep to make his acquaintance for the first time. As it happened, these two very different characters hit it off. As soon as Buckingham met Fairfax's daughter, Mary, he was very clear on what he would do. He immediately began to woo the not very beautiful Mary, with considerable success. Mary's plain looks did not seem to bother the man who was described as the 'most graceful and beautiful person that any Court in Europe ever saw'.[24]

He wrote to Mary's mother in the following fashion:

. . . if your ladiship knew the nature of the passion I have for her, you could not be soe ill-natured (however averse to mee soever she might bee) as not to pitty my condition or to refuse the endeavouring to further mee by your favour to the enjoying of what only in this world can make mee perfectly happy. That is Madame, the honour of being your Ladyship's most dutifull son . . .[25]

Among his papers is a note probably written to Mary at the time:

The little Ribbon I received from you last night instead of binding up my wound, has made it greater, and though I have kept it ever since as neere my heart as I cowld, I can finde noe other effects by it, then the being much lesse at my ease then I was before. I have not slept one wink never since I saw you, neither have I beene able to thinke of any other thinge then how to finde the meanes of speakinge to your Deare Mistrisse, for I dare not without her leave presume to call her myne, though it bee already owt of my power ever to call justly soe anybody else.[26]

Buckingham's skill at conviviality was not all expended on the Fairfax family, however, for at the same time he also managed to build up a friendship with the children of Oliver Cromwell, paying them many visits and enjoying their hospitality. They no doubt enjoyed his vivacity and capacity for entertainment. His gamble on coming to England in this way was rewarded when Cromwell decided not to have him arrested.

Buckingham and Lady Mary Fairfax were married on 7

September 1657 by a Presbyterian, Mr Vere Harcourt, who was impressed enough by the Duke to state that he saw God in his face.[27] Shortly after the marriage, however, things took a bad turn for the newly-weds when it became known that Buckingham was to be arrested. His new father-in-law, Lord Fairfax, sought an audience with Cromwell himself and his influence resulted in the Duke being confined to the luxury of York House. In characteristic style Buckingham refused to stay a prisoner and, using his skill of disguise, began to go on various trips including one to visit his sister. When he was captured on one of these audacious excursions Cromwell was angry enough to have him thrown in the Tower, and this time Lord Fairfax's intercessions fell on deaf ears.

Buckingham was still languishing in the Tower and fearing for his life when the news came through of Cromwell's death:

> . . . I was then close prisoner in the Tower, with a couple of Guards lying always in my chamber and a sentinel at my door. I confess I was not a little delighted with the noise of the great guns, for I presently knew what it meant, and if Oliver had lived for three days longer I had certainly been put to death.[28]

Under the rule of Richard Cromwell Buckingham's situation became easier. He was moved to Windsor, where he 'became a rallying point for the crew of reckless conspirators, who ever gravitated toward the Duke'.[29] On 21 February 1659 Lord Fairfax put forward a petition for his release to the House of Commons. He offered to be personally responsible for the Duke. One of those who spoke on Buckingham's behalf was Sir Anthony Ashley Cooper, the future Lord Shaftesbury and 'Achitophel' of Dryden's famous poem.[30] More than anything it was the respect in which Lord Fairfax was held by the House that won the day. The House decided that

George Villiers, Duke of Buckingham now a prisoner at Windsor Castle, upon his engagement and upon his honour, at the Bar of the House and upon the engagement of the Lord Fairfax in £20,000, that the said Duke shall peaceable demean himself for the future, and shall not join with nor abet or have any correspondence with any of the enemies of the Lord Protector of the Commonwealth . . . [31]

It is clear that Lord Fairfax was acting more out of love for his daughter than out of any confidence in the morals of the Duke of Buckingham. 'When I engage my estate I know what I do,' he said, 'but when I engage his honour, I engage what is not in my power.'[32] In any event Buckingham was freed and returned to live with his wife in her father's house at Nun Appleton.

With the restoration of the monarchy in the person of Charles II, Buckingham was looking forward to a bright future, 'a vision of power such as few subjects save his own father had wielded, rose before him'.[33] He was in an enviable position, having property, money, youth and, thanks to his upbringing, a close intimacy with the new King. He had also played his part, alongside his father-in-law, in fighting the King's cause in the months leading up to the Restoration. However, it must have come as a shock to the Duke when in comparison with other former offenders he was greeted by Charles with a coldness on his arrival in England. Undeterred, Buckingham continued to attempt to ingratiate himself with the King. He made sure to meet him nightly at the lodgings of his cousin, the King's mistress, Barbara Villiers.

In 1661 Buckingham's interest in affairs of the heart once again got the better of him when, unknown to his wife, he became infatuated with Princess Henrietta, the King's younger sister. However, this young lady was to marry her cousin, the brother of Louis XIV, Philippe, the duc d'Orléans. So besotted with her was Buckingham that he even contrived to get permission to accompany the

Princess and the Queen Mother as they made their journey to France. As it happened, the unfortunate Princess became very ill with measles on the way and for a time was in danger of dying. So pained by this was Buckingham that his behaviour at the time is described as that of a 'lunatic'.[34] The Queen Mother noticed his irrational behaviour towards the Princess and ordered him to go on to Paris ahead of them.

However, when they all finally reached their destination and met with the duc d'Orléans, Buckingham's behaviour did not improve. In fact it became so bad that the Queen Mother decided to contact Charles and have him write to Buckingham to warn him off and get him to leave. When he received the order, although the Duke had no option but to leave, he did so most reluctantly and only 'after a thousand lingering farewells and renewed protestations of love and devotion'.[35]

Although somewhat out of favour at Charles's coronation, Buckingham was given the honour of carrying the orb before the new king. His new suit for the occasion is reputed to have cost him a remarkable £30,000.[36] Soon afterwards he was made Lord Lieutenant of Yorkshire.

It was around this time that Buckingham began what he probably started as nothing more than a strategy to ingratiate himself with the King. He befriended Frances Stuart, who was a renowned beauty at court and well known to be beloved of the King. *La belle Stuart*, as she was known, was a Scotswoman who was maid of honour to the Queen and it was common knowledge at court that Charles was very much in love with her. There is no doubt that she was very fond of Buckingham and in particular enjoyed his sense of humour. So fond of his company was she in fact that if he failed to arrive at her apartment on a particular evening she would send for him.[37] However, it all ended badly when he declared his love for her and she felt compelled to reject him, thereby bringing their friendship to an end.

Apart from Buckingham's affairs of the heart and his literary pursuits he somehow also found time to become involved in manufacturing. In 1663 he took out a patent for extracting glass and crystals from flint and set up a factory at Lambeth, manufacturing 'huge vases of metall as cleare, ponderous, and thicke as crystal; also looking-glasses far larger and better than any that come from Venice'.[38]

Buckingham identified two major hate figures whom he blamed for his estrangement from the King. He believed firmly that as long as these two rivals, Clarendon and Ormonde, were in power his chances of political progress would be severely retarded. He began to make himself the focal point for anyone who held a grudge against either of these two men. He was thus not pleased when his sister, Mary, Duchess of Richmond, betrothed her daughter, also called Mary, to Richard, Earl of Arran, a son of the Duke of Ormonde. To make matters worse, since after seven years Buckingham's own marriage had not brought forth children, the Duke of Ormonde saw fit to send him a note requesting that the Villiers' estates be settled on his son Richard's new wife.

The Irish Cattle Bill of 1666 brought the bad feelings between the Duke and the Ormondes to the surface. Buckingham viewed the Bill, which sought to ban the importation of Irish cattle to England, as an opportunity to bring about Ormonde's downfall, such would be its effect on the economy of Ireland. He therefore supported it passionately and so found himself in direct conflict with Ormonde's son, Ossory.

As if the public disagreement with Ossory had not been damaging enough to his reputation, a few days later Buckingham was involved in yet another petty altercation. Both Houses of Parliament were crowded together in joint session when Buckingham gave offence to the Marquis of Dorchester by resting his elbow on him. When the Marquis rebuked him the Duke gave as good as he got. A scuffle ensued between these two aristocrats, during which Buckingham pulled off the Marquis's wig and the Marquis pulled out a lump of the Duke's hair. Such was the outrage that once again Buckingham found himself incarcerated in the Tower, as did the Marquis. After a few days, and once they had agreed to make friends, they were both freed.[39] Buckingham made his position even worse some time later when he broke protocol by brazenly arriving at Whitehall without first entreating the King's forgiveness. For this latest indiscretion he found himself banished from Court.

His decline was not to end there, however. A few years earlier in 1663 Braythwaite, the manager of Buckingham's estates, had been threatened with arrest on suspicion of plotting. At that time the Duke had persuaded Charles to interview the man personally. Charles seems to have been enthralled by this rogue, a trait that would appear again later when dealing with Blood. After the interview Braythwaite was released on condition that he become a spy for the King. Ironically, in 1667 he came to the King with information about his employer. He said that Buckingham was colluding in secret with men 'of very desperate intentions'.[40] This was very bad news for the Duke, coming as it did after his recent scandals and considering how he was disliked by such powerful people as Clarendon, Ormonde and also Lord Arlington.[41] Buckingham's situation at the time was not helped either by some animosity felt towards him by his cousin Barbara.[42]

Yet things were to get even worse. Pursuing his interest in the occult, Buckingham had become acquainted with one Dr John Heydon, an astrologer and member of the religious sect known as the Rosicrucian Circle. This man was known to have been involved previously in plots against the King.[43] In 1664 he had been imprisoned for debt and was only released as a result of Buckingham's influence. During the Cromwellian regime Cromwell's son Richard had paid Heydon a visit in disguise, only to hear the prediction that his father would be hanged. Not only was he mistaken about the hanging but Heydon also got the date of death wrong by four years. He spent sixteen months in prison for making it.[44] In 1667 Heydon was arrested for conspiracy and Arlington claimed to have found amongst his papers a horoscope of the King's life which had been commissioned by the Duke of Buckingham.[45] According to the law of the time, casting a horoscope of the King was an act of treason. The King was furious and ordered Buckingham's arrest. However, when the soldiers arrived to arrest the Duke he defended his house for some time before managing to escape.

The King issued a proclamation threatening 'all severity to those who would harbour or conceal him'.[46] Buckingham was also removed from the Privy Council and the Lord Lieutenancy of York. He went into hiding and was not found, though it was said that he was arrested at one point for rioting in London and because he was not recognised was released.[47]

There is a chance that on this occasion Buckingham may have been innocent of the charges laid against him and that they had been fabricated by his enemies. One Mrs Damport on examination at the time did make a disturbing statement about the activities of a man called Middleton: 'Middleton did confese that he had received £100 from my Lord Arlington to bear witness against the Duke for having the King's nativity cast by Heydon, and to testify he heard the Duke speake treason against the King and the Government'.[48] She went on to declare that another man, whom she called Fryr, was paid £60 for his evidence and that both were to receive £500 when it was all over. According to her, Middleton told her daughter that there was no truth in the accusation and that he only did it for the money.

For some time the King was unmoved by the requests for forgiveness that came from Buckingham and his friends. Such was his anger that he even publicly blamed the Duke and his followers for the continuance of the war against the

Dutch, saying that they had not supported him in his efforts to bring the enemy to submission.[49]

The actions of Ormonde and Clarendon at the time did nothing to alleviate the animosity between them and Buckingham. Clarendon had actively encouraged the King to have Buckingham arrested and while the Duke was on the run he refused a request from him for an interview to resolve the issue. Ormonde wrote a letter to Clarendon at the time in which he reminded him that, if the Duke's offence 'prove capitall', Buckingham's niece, his son Lord Arran's wife, was innocent of any crime and should not suffer in her inheritance.[50]

By July, however, circumstances had improved vastly for Buckingham. He had put things right with Barbara, and the witness who had brought the main accusation against him was dead. He decided that the best course of action to take now was to hand himself in to the authorities and deny the charges outright. He did this and was remanded to the Tower. A Select Commission was established to examine his case and, as one would expect, the Duke proved a confident and ebullient defendant. During his examination he admitted that although he was acquainted with Dr Heydon he 'tooke him to be soe silly a fellow that I would not thinke it fitt to trust him with a tallow candle'.[51] He denied that he had played a part in any treasonable act. He was eventually cleared of the charges and it was not long until he was once again greeting the King at Barbara's lodgings and, although the King was cold at first, cordiality between them was soon restored. However, it might be an overstatement to say, as one writer has, that 'from a hunted fugitive, Buckingham rapidly developed into the Sovereign's chief friend and adviser'.[52]

Made even more determined by his recent experiences, it was from this improved situation that Buckingham began to use any influence he had with the King to attack his enemies, Clarendon and Ormonde. He was aided and abetted in this endeavour by Barbara, whose hatred for them was equal to his own. Also deeply involved in the attack on Clarendon, and perhaps even more influential, were William Coventry and Lord Arlington.[53] The King, who had been under Clarendon's influence since his youth, was also becoming convinced that it was time for a change. When the attack on Clarendon came it was publicly fronted by Coventry and Arlington. As they attacked him in Parliament a mob smashed his windows. By August 1667 their efforts yielded fruit when Clarendon was forced to surrender the Great Seal of office. He was impeached by the House of Commons, charged with a list of crimes including cruelty in office, disclosing state secrets, intending to introduce military government in England, insolence to the King and mismanaging the war. In the end only the support of the House of Lords saved his life. Eventually the unfortunate man, who had taken the recent death of his wife very badly, was hounded into exile in France, where he died in 1674.

Buckingham's aim had been to improve his own political position with the removal of Clarendon. It has been claimed that 'the power that the Chancellor had wielded now for the most part devolved on Buckingham. . . . he was practically the Prime Minister of the new administration'.[54] Actually, historians disagree on the extent of Buckingham's personal power after the removal of Clarendon.[55] But the collective influence of that political clique known as the CABAL (i.e. Clifford, Ashley, Buckingham, Arlington, Lauderdale) was undoubtedly increased.

On the personal side, however, things were not going so well for Buckingham. By this time the marriage was becoming ever more difficult for his wife Mary. Rumours of the Duke's infidelities had been rife for some time and we can only surmise that his wife must have been aware of them. With the emergence of his new-found power it seems he did even less to hide his adulterous lifestyle. In July 1667 he had an open fight with Harry Killigrew, the former lover of his mistress, the Countess of Shrewsbury, in which he injured the young man quite badly. This event caused such gossip that the Countess's husband felt obliged to challenge Buckingham to a duel. On the assigned day Buckingham wounded the unfortunate man badly, 'the sword entering by the right breast and coming out at the shoulder'.[56] Such was the interest in the duel that reports were circulated at the time, most probably fabricated, in which it was claimed that the woman whose love was at issue, Lady Shrewsbury, had witnessed the whole event in disguise and even ran to her lover at the end to congratulate him, carrying the bloodstained shirt of her husband in her hand. Furthermore, it was said that on her person she had concealed two pistols, intending to kill her husband and herself should Buckingham die in the fight.[57]

When the unfortunate husband died some two months later, the surgeons who performed the post mortem declared that his wound from the duel had already healed and consequently was not the cause of his death. However, Buckingham had already ensured that he was granted a King's pardon, which protected him against any charges arising out of the duel. This bending of the law by the King caused an outcry at the time, so much so in fact that Charles felt the need to make the public assurance that 'on no pretence whatsoever any pardon shall hereafter be granted to any person whatsoever for killing of any man in any duel . . . but that the course of law shall wholly take place in all such cases'.[58]

Even this did not bring Buckingham's bad behaviour to an end. His next act was to brazenly bring Shrewsbury's widow to live in his house alongside his wife. When Mary complained about it, his reply was that there was a coach available to take her to her father's house if she so wished.[59]

Undeterred by any scandal in his private life, Buckingham arrived for business at the opening of Parliament in February 1668. One of his first aims was to tackle the persecution being felt by the Protestant Nonconformist community, but the Toleration Act proposed by him was rejected by a majority of members. One of his long-held ambitions did come to fruition, however, when in 1669 Ormonde was removed from the Lord Lieutenancy of Ireland. But, much to Buckingham's chagrin and contrary to his hopes, this was not followed by his own appointment to the position.

Although the main target for Buckingham's political vindictiveness had become the Duke of Ormonde, he also found time to play a role in the political downfall of William Coventry. His attitude towards Coventry may have been determined by the fact that as Joint Commissioner of the Treasury he had been one of those on a Select Commission sent to examine Buckingham when he was held in the Tower as a result of the Heydon affair.[60] Coventry himself had played his part in the destruction of Clarendon's political career. The demise of Coventry was initiated by the production of a play in which his character was lampooned, written by none other than Buckingham. Coventry complained to the King, but when the text of the play was shown to His Majesty the offending scene had been removed and Charles could find no fault with it. The whole affair left Coventry frustrated and very angry with Buckingham and as a result he challenged the Duke to a duel. For this act he found himself dismissed from office and imprisoned briefly in the Tower in 1669. Such was his disillusionment over the whole affair that he never took high office again, although he remained in Parliament until its dissolution in 1679.[61]

Buckingham's political focus switched to foreign affairs when he became involved in negotiations on an alliance with Louis XIV's France. He was not to know that he was actually being used as a pawn by the King as Charles investigated the possibility of converting to Roman Catholicism. The Duke's sister, the Duchess of Richmond, had warned him in a letter, writing that she had heard of negotiations taking place without his knowledge between the King, the King's sister Henrietta and Louis. Perhaps it was Buckingham's deep affection for Henrietta that prevented him from seeing the truth. Henrietta managed to assuage his fears on the matter by appealing to his ego and telling him how much Louis depended on him: '. . . he has told me he would give up the whole thing, if the Duke were to change his mind'. At no time did Charles let Buckingham know of his real intention or his desire to convert to Roman Catholicism.[62] Buckingham's well-known devotion to Protestantism made him the ideal cover for the King's covert negotiations. No one would believe that the Duke could be a party to such 'papist' activities.

In 1670 Henrietta came on a visit to her homeland and obtained Charles's signature to the secret Treaty of Dover, of which Buckingham knew nothing.[63] Under this treaty Charles pledged support for a war against Holland in return for some territory, and he also agreed to recognise any future claim by Louis to the Spanish crown. But most scandalously he also agreed, in return for two million French crowns, to publicly convert to Roman Catholicism.

Princess Henrietta returned to France with the treaty, only to die shortly afterwards, to the deep sorrow of both her brother and Buckingham. For a time foul play was suspected but the post mortem categorically ruled this out. Shortly afterwards the Duke found himself in France innocently and earnestly continuing what were in fact sham negotiations towards a treaty. He was convinced that everything was going well and Louis encouraged this enthusiasm by making him feel indispensable to the process. No wonder he felt as he did when, on leaving, he was presented with a sword and belt worth 40,000 crowns, a promise to grant Lady Shrewsbury 10,000 livres a year, and an assurance that he would be awarded a military command in the Low Countries.

In reality, two Treaties of Dover were signed in 1670, one the secret document under which Charles agreed to convert to Roman Catholicism as soon as circumstances would permit, and another making no reference to such a clause. This public treaty, signed at the end of the year, has been described as nothing more than a 'cover-up'.[64] Buckingham and the four other members of the CABAL signed this public treaty. It seems that only Clifford and Arlington knew of the existence of the secret version.[65] This secret treaty even had a clause rendering the public one null and void in advance, but as time went on Charles began to invent excuses to delay his promised religious conversion.

In the end the Duke never got the military command he had been promised, that position instead being given to the King's son, the Duke of Monmouth. Buckingham was furious about this and let the King know how he felt. He was firmly reprimanded by Charles, who told him that 'he was worth no more than a dog if he conflicted with the public good'.[66]

While he was involved in these weighty affairs of state the scandal attached to Buckingham's private life continued to escalate. One night in 1669 Harry Killigrew, the competitor for Lady Shrewbury's affections, was attacked and badly wounded and his attendant murdered. It seems that Lady Shrewsbury was present to watch the event from a carriage. Killigrew survived his injuries and Buckingham made a public statement in which he claimed that someone who had witnessed the event, a person he did not name, had told him that it was Killigrew who had started the fight and that his opponents had meant only to 'cudgel him'.[67]

The public humiliation of Buckingham's wife must have been at its most painful when it became common knowledge that Lady Shrewsbury had given birth to the Duke of Buckingham's son. It is obvious that Buckingham felt no shame over the matter as he gave the child the spurious title Earl of Coventry and even held a lavish baptismal ceremony at which the King acted as godfather. Unfortunately the poor child was to die soon afterwards and the subsequent funeral held at Westminster Abbey was 'a princely pageant, where kings-at-arms and pursuivants trumpeted the poor babe's fictitious titles, before consigning the little coffin to its last resting-place, amongst the ashes of our Sovereigns, in Henry VII.'s Chapel'.[68]

It was around this time also that, because of the history of enmity between the two dukes, suspicion began to fall on Buckingham as to the role he played in Blood's infamous attack on the life of the Duke of Ormonde. Many believed that Blood had been working for Buckingham. Ormonde himself was under no illusion about how Buckingham regarded him and in a letter to his son described him as a 'vile man'.[69] Certainly Ormonde's son, the Earl of Ossory, believed there was substance to the claims being made about Buckingham's involvement in the attack. So much so, in fact, that he decided to confront Buckingham directly on the issue. He did so when he saw the Duke standing right beside the King.

My lord, I know well that you are at the bottom of this late attempt of Blood's upon my father; and therefore I give you fair warning; if my father come to a violent end by sword or pistol, if he dies by the hand of a ruffian, or by the more secret way of poison, I shall not be at a loss to know the first author of it; I shall consider you as the assassin; I shall treat you as such; and wherever I meet you I shall pistol you, though you stood behind the king's chair; and I tell it you in his majesty's presence, that you may be sure I shall keep my word.[70]

Buckingham, it seems, was so taken aback by this direct approach that uncharacteristically for him he did not reply. We can only wonder if these candid comments had anything to do with the fact that no further attempts were made on Ormonde's life. However, Buckingham's association with Blood did not end there.

10

THE CROWN JEWELS

The first English king who thought it necessary to place his collection of jewels under special protection was Edward the Confessor, who entrusted them to the care of the monks of Westminster Abbey. The King's treasure was kept there in the Pyx Chamber. During the reign of Henry III it was decided to move the most valuable items such as the Crown and Sceptre to the Tower of London for safe keeping, where they were most probably housed in the White Tower. A person known as the Keeper of the Regalia, whose responsibility it was to safeguard the collection, was also appointed. During the reign of Edward I a portion of the Crown Jewels, which still remained at Westminster Abbey, was stolen, as a result of which the Abbot and forty-eight monks spent two years imprisoned in the Tower.[1] After that it was decided to move the complete collection to the Tower.

By the time of Elizabeth I's reign the Crown Jewels were housed in a purpose-built Jewel House adjoining the White Tower. The valuables remained there in safe keeping throughout the reign of James I and up to the execution of Charles I.

During the years of Cromwell's rule 'all regal emblems were broken up, destroyed, or sold for what they would fetch'.[2] Almost every piece of the Coronation Regalia was sold off or melted down, only three swords and the Coronation Spoon surviving. With the restoration of the monarchy it became necessary to remake most of the collection. This responsibility fell to Sir Robert Vyner, who was the Court Jeweller at that time. Part of Vyner's duty was to make these new pieces as much like the old as possible from the detailed records that still survived. The total bill for all the replacements came to the substantial sum of £32,000.[3] By this time the Jewel House itself had also fallen into disrepair and the basement floor of the Martin Tower was chosen as the place to house this new collection.

Throughout Charles II's reign many visitors were led through the only door into this thick-walled room to admire the beautiful treasures on display. Of prime interest to any visitor to the Martin Tower would have been those items referred to as the Regalia, which were used during the coronation ceremony. Chief among these was St Edward's Crown, also known as the Crown of England. This is the crown depicted standing on the shield in the arms of England. The original, which got its name from its first owner, Edward the Confessor, dated from around the year 1042, when he became King. Since that had been destroyed under Cromwell, visitors to the Tower during the reign of Charles II would have been admiring Vyner's replacement. It has been claimed that the new crown was built on a surviving element of the old one. This new crown weighed nearly five pounds and was made of gold with red, blue, green and yellow stones set all around the band. Under ancient law it was not permitted to take St Edward's Crown outside the British Isles. During the coronation ceremony it would be placed briefly on the new monarch's head before being replaced by the lighter King's State Crown.

Visitors to the Martin Tower could admire the King's State Crown, which was used at all state occasions throughout the reign. Members of the public could not have failed to notice the large gem, known as the Black

Prince's Ruby, which was set into it. In fact this is not a ruby at all but a semi-precious stone known as a spinel. It first belonged to the eldest son of King Edward III, known as the Black Prince. Edward III had lent a force of four or five thousand men to Don Pedro, the King of Castille, for a war he was fighting in Spain. The Black Prince went as a part of this force and as a sign of gratitude for his fighting efforts Don Pedro presented him with this substantial ruby. It had something of a bloody past since Don Pedro had got the ruby by killing the King of Granada and taking it from him. It passed on from monarch to monarch, even being worn on the helmet of Henry V at the battle of Agincourt, where it narrowly escaped being damaged.[4] The ruby was ignominiously sold off for a mere £4 during the Commonwealth to an unknown purchaser but eventually made its way back to join the rest of the Crown Jewels and was set proudly into this new State Crown for Charles II.

Among other pieces of the Regalia on display was the royal sceptre, also made by Sir Robert Vyner. This valuable staff with a cross on top was made to symbolise the King's temporal power under the cross. It was three feet long and set with many jewels. Then there was the orb, also made by Vyner for Charles II, which consisted of a gold globe, again with a cross standing on top. Around the centre of this orb Vyner had set rubies, sapphires, emeralds and diamonds. On one side of the cross was an emerald and on the other a sapphire; both were surrounded by diamonds. The orb, which cost £1,150, was only ever placed in the hands of the sovereign of the realm and signified 'the domination of the Christian religion over the world'.[5] Apart from the wonders of the Regalia there would have been many other fine pieces to admire, such as the royal plate, salt cellars, wine fountains and spoons.

The Keeper of the Jewel House during the reign of Charles II was Sir Gilbert Talbot, appointed by the King after his restoration. In a document dated 1680 Talbot outlined the rights and perquisites that had traditionally belonged to the office.[6] As well as a salary of £50 a year the Keeper lived rent-free at apartments in all the King's palaces and at the Tower of London. He also received food to the amount of 'fourteen double dishes per diem' and 'as much beer, wine and spirits as seemed good unto him'.[7] Every year the King would receive what was known as his New Year gift money. This was usually £3,000 in gold given to him by the nobility. It was received by the Keeper and out of it he was entitled to keep one shilling in the pound and also to keep any profit which accrued from exchanging the gold for silver. He made around £300 a year from this source. He also made another £300 a year from tips received when presenting gifts to foreign ambassadors. It was also his right to appoint the goldsmiths and jewellers to the king and queen, for which the firm chosen would pay him £800. Among other things he was also entitled to a close wagon for his own goods and two carts for his officers, robes at the coronation and the right to his place in procession before all judges. He alone had the right to place the crown on the monarch's head or remove it.

However, when Talbot took up the position he complained that many of these privileges had been encroached upon by the Lord Chancellor, Hyde. For example, instead of his food and drink allowance as outlined above, he was now receiving only £120 a year in its place. He was also unhappy with the amount he was receiving out of the New Year gift money; as a result the King fixed this amount at £400.

Once a coronation ceremony was over, all the pieces of the Regalia would be handed back to the Keeper of the Jewel House for safe return to the Tower of London. It was his duty to travel around with the King and be responsible for the various parts of the regalia that the King needed on a trip. If at any time the King required his State Crown, the Keeper would bring it to him, place it on the sovereign's head and return it intact to the Tower afterwards.

In 1671, since the main place of residence of Sir Gilbert Talbot was the Palace at Whitehall, the responsibility for the day-to-day protection of the collection while it was in the Tower fell to the Assistant Keeper of the Jewel House. The holder of this position was one Talbot Edwards, who was seventy-seven years of age at the time. Edwards was permitted to live with his wife and daughter above the collection in the Martin Tower.

Since Edwards's remuneration for the job was not substantial, and in any event he had not managed to draw it for many years from what was an impoverished exchequer, he was permitted by the King to charge admittance fees for people to see the Jewels. He would guide people to the ground floor of the Martin Tower and into the room where they could gaze upon the Regalia. These items were on display in a cupboard that had been specially made from a recess in the thick wall with a cross-wired door for ease of viewing. As Edwards went about his daily business he did not know that he was about to have his most unforgettable visitor.

11

AN UNFORGETTABLE VISITOR

We do not know when exactly Blood turned his attention to his next adventure, but at some stage he began to formulate an ambitious plan to infiltrate the Tower of London and steal the Crown Jewels. Although the security measures in place at the Tower in the seventeenth century were nothing like those in use today, it still posed an intimidating target for any potential robber. Surrounded by two rows of massive walls and a deep moat, it was protected by the Yeoman of the Guard and a battalion of the King's Guard. Nevertheless, having assessed the situation, Blood obviously felt that the odds were in his favour. From his observations he would have been aware that many civilians lived in the confines of the Tower and that a multitude of people passed in and out of there every day without notice. In addition there were no guards actually at the site of the Jewels and, at seventy-seven, Edwards, the Assistant Keeper, could be overcome without too much difficulty.

About three weeks before the robbery Blood came to see the Crown Jewels disguised as a clergyman and accompanied by a woman whom he introduced as his wife. Although the woman he described as such was not his real wife, she played the role admirably. She may have been a young actress named Jenny Blaine.[1] Edwards later described the clergyman as having a long beard and wearing a cap with ears, a cassock and a long cloak. As ever, Edwards was delighted to show the collection to paying visitors and led them directly to the basement of the Martin Tower. Once Blood had carefully surveyed the beauty of the Regalia and the other pieces on display, his 'wife' suddenly felt ill or, as Edwards described it, had 'a qualm upon her stomack'.[2] The old man hurried to fetch her a drink. Mrs Edwards returned with the drink and brought the woman upstairs to rest upon a bed for a few minutes. Blood's 'wife' was not too ill, for she recovered fairly quickly and both she and her clergyman husband left, thanking the Edwards most graciously for their kindness.

Of course the matter did not end there. A few days later Blood, once again playing the role of the clergyman, returned with a present of four pairs of gloves for Mrs Edwards as a token of his appreciation. Other visits followed, as did much convivial conversation until Blood had managed to build up a warm relationship with the Edwards. Once this relationship had developed sufficiently he announced one day that he wished to advance a mutually beneficial proposal. As the Edwards listened attentively he told them that he wished to propose a match between his own nephew and their very beautiful daughter. Such was their respect and liking for the clergyman and his wife that the Edwards were well disposed towards the proposed marriage from the beginning. They might also of course have been influenced by Blood's statement 'that his nephew had two or three hundred a year in land'.[3] In any event a dinner was arranged, to be held at the Martin Tower, during which both parties would discuss the matter further.

The dinner proved a great success and Edwards later recounted how he remembered the reverend gentleman saying a number of prayers both before and after their meal, including some for the King, the Queen and the royal family! After dinner Edwards gave Blood a tour of the premises, and the good clergyman even bought a case of pistols from him that he had admired as they hung on the wall. He said that the arms were to be a gift for a young nobleman of his acquaintance, but of course the purchase had the rather convenient effect of removing the pistols from the Tower.

The date fixed upon for the nephew to be brought to the Martin Tower to meet his intended bride was 9 May 1671. At 7 a.m. on the day in question Thomas Blood, once again disguised as the clergyman, his son, alias Tom Hunt, and two other criminal associates, Robert Perrott, a Baptist and one-time Cromwellian soldier who was now a silk-dyer, and Richard Halliwell, all arrived at the Martin Tower.[4] It is possible that one other gang member had remained outside the formidable walls of the complex to take care of the horses. This man could have been William Smith, a known Fifth Monarchist.[5] Knowing that they would not be searched on entering the Tower, they were all armed with swordsticks, daggers and pistols. Halliwell remained at the door of the Martin Tower to keep watch while Blood, his son and Perrott went inside. Although the intended bride did not come down herself at this time, curiosity must have got the better of her because she did send her maid to catch a glimpse of her intended husband. The maid, seeing the look-out man, supposed him to be the nephew and ran upstairs again to give her mistress a detailed description of her suitor.[6]

Blood, having given his greetings, casually suggested that while they awaited the arrival of the ladies his friends might like to see the Crown Jewels. The Assistant Keeper, no doubt thinking of his fee, complied willingly. But as soon as the poor man had led them into the basement room they threw a cloak over his head and stuffed a piece of wood with an air hole in it into his mouth. As the startled old man began to struggle they told him that if he behaved himself he would not be harmed. When he refused to comply, they hit him several times with a wooden mallet, causing him to fall to the floor. Blood later told how he stopped one of his men from killing Edwards there and then. But still the old man refused to stay quiet, so they beat him again and finally stabbed him in the stomach.[7] One of the robbers knelt down to listen to his breathing and concluded that he was in fact dead. Although Edwards was not dead he thought it wise to allow them to think he was.

Blood now surveyed the Crown Jewels that lay unprotected before him behind the cross-wired door. He deliberated between the two crowns, St Edward's and the King's State Crown, the sceptre, the orb and the other pieces. Forcing open the light door he chose to target some major pieces of the Regalia. He picked up the lighter of the two crowns, the King's State Crown, and, using the wooden mallet, battered it until it fitted inside the small bag that was hidden under his cloak. This caused some of the precious stones to be dislodged, including the Black Prince's Ruby. Most of the fallen stones were quickly and unceremoniously gathered from the floor and stuffed into various pockets, among them the Black Prince's Ruby. Perrott then picked up the orb and hid it inside his trousers, while Blood junior began to file the sceptre in half hurriedly, so that it could be carried out unnoticed.

Just then the jewel thieves were disturbed by their accomplice Halliwell, who rushed in to tell them that a man purporting to be the Assistant Keeper's son had just arrived and had gone upstairs to see his family. It is a strange coincidence that Edwards's son, who had been at war on the continent and had not been at home for ten years,[8] should have arrived home at that particular moment. Blood and his men knew that the son would soon join them in the basement and decided to flee immediately, taking only the State Crown and the orb with them. The partly filed sceptre was left behind on the floor.

No sooner had they left the basement than old Edwards began to shout, 'Treason! Murder!' His daughter was the first to find him and she ran out into the parade ground shouting at the top of her voice, 'Treason! The crown is stolen!'[9] Pursuit was soon given by Edwards's son. He was accompanied on the chase by Captain Martin Beckman, who had been invited to the Tower so that he could be present at the betrothal. Beckman was a Swedish-born military engineer of rather dubious character who had worked both as a mercenary soldier and as a spy. After a very varied career, including a spell spent as a prisoner in the Tower, he had been appointed Third Engineer of the State in 1670.[10]

In the mean time Blood's son and Halliwell had passed safely through the outer gate and were preparing to ride away. Blood and Perrott had passed the Bloody Tower and were just making their way along Water Lane approaching Byward Tower when their pursuers spotted them and called out to the Yeoman on duty at the drawbridge to capture them. However, when the man tried to do so, Blood fired a shot at him, which although it missed him caused him to lie on the ground. As they ran over the drawbridge, a guardsman named Sill who was standing on the other side beside the Middle Tower simply stepped out of their way, perhaps in fear or because he had been paid off in advance. Blood and Perrott should then have taken the obvious route of exiting through the Bulwark Gate but decided instead to double back towards the Iron Gate. This decision brought them along the very open and busy wharf.

As they made their way through the crowds Blood and Perrott found that young Edwards and Beckman were gaining on them. Blood decided to create a diversion and managed to cause considerable confusion by audaciously yelling 'Stop thief!' to the crowd, gesturing as he did so towards his pursuers. With this, some public-spirited individuals jumped upon the two young men and Beckman in particular was lucky to escape uninjured. Eventually, however, they managed to establish their innocence and continue with the chase. Beckman was the first to catch up with Blood and Perrott as they were about to mount some horses. Blood, seeing him approach, fired on him but missed. They then began to struggle over the crown until help arrived and both Blood and Perrott were subdued. The Black Prince's Ruby, which had become dislodged from the crown after its ill-treatment, was discovered in Perrott's pocket.[11] Meanwhile Blood's son was in such haste to get away from the scene of the crime that he rode his horse into a turning cart and was thrown to the ground. As he tried to remount he was recognised by a cobbler as Thomas Hunt the outlaw 'who was in this bloody business against the Duke of Ormonde' and was promptly arrested.[12] He was soon imprisoned in the Tower with his father and Perrott.

The reasons why Blood decided to embark upon this daring attempt to rob the Crown Jewels have often been pondered. It has frequently been assumed that his motive was simply common theft, an attempt to profit financially. Indeed he added to this belief himself by claiming to have been misinformed about the value of the jewels. He commented to the King, rather impertinently, that when he stole the crown he believed it to have been worth a hundred thousand pounds when in fact, as he subsequently found out, the whole Regalia had cost considerably less.[13] But we have no other example of his committing a crime for financial gain. In fact the whole idea of this sort of criminality seems to run contrary to his deeply felt religious beliefs. As already noted he described his son's engagement in similar criminality as 'My sonn's wickedness'.[14]

Many wondered if he had been working on behalf of the Duke of Buckingham. After all, there were strong suspicions, not least on the part of the Earl of Ossory, that he had been doing so when he kidnapped the Duke of Ormonde. Buckingham was believed to have harboured some fantastical political ambitions of usurping the King. The theft of the Crown could have been intended as a first step towards the assassination of the King and the ascent of Buckingham to the throne. His staunch Protestantism meant that Buckingham was opposed to the accession of the Roman Catholic Duke of York. He also believed firmly that since his mother was a descendant of Edward IV his Plantagenet bloodline gave him more right to the throne than any bastard son of Charles, such as Monmouth.[15] The rumour, although fanciful, was given further credibility by the fact that an attempt was made to steal the Great Seal from the Chancellor's house at around the same time.

However, it is much more likely that for Blood the stealing of the Crown Jewels was, just like all his other acts, politically motivated. A theft such as this from under the eyes of the authorities would have had considerable symbolic significance, rather like the capture of Dublin Castle or the kidnap of the Duke of Ormonde. After a number of failed plots, the theft of the Crown would have had great propaganda value. It would have focused much attention on the cause of Protestant Nonconformists and may have convinced the authorities that they would have no peace until some form of religious toleration was granted. In addition, according to a contemporary source, the attack on Ormonde had not been very popular among Blood's own community and he had lost some support as a result of it: 'those congregations of Nonconformists which they have formerly frequented abhor this fact, and would be glad to bring them to punishment if it were in their power'.[16] Blood may have hoped that an audacious act of defiance such as the theft of the Crown Jewels from the Tower of London would reinstate him in their affections.

We cannot discount another motivation in the attempt. A part of Blood would be drawn to an act such as this by the pure risk and daring involved. For a man in his circumstances, wanted by the authorities and who could so easily have been incarcerated in the Tower, to have the nerve to consider robbing the place is evidence of a certain recklessness. There is no doubt that such a theft would appeal to his nature. As one biographer puts it, 'he knew the Enterprize would make such a noise in the world, that he was sure to be another Herostratus, and to live in story for the strangeness, if not the success of his attempts'.[17]

The Tower of London was a tough prison in the seventeenth century and both Blood and his son, like so many others, must have found the conditions difficult. There is an indication of this in a petition dated June 1671: 'Petition of Thomas Blood, senior, to Lord Arlington that his health being impaired by close confinement in the Tower, his wife may be allowed access to him'.[18] A similarly worded document pleaded that Thomas junior also be allowed to see his mother. From the outside Maria also petitioned to be allowed visiting rights: 'Petition of Mary, [Maria] wife of Thomas Blood, to Lord Arlington, for access to her Husband and eldest son, who have been now near eight weeks so closely imprisoned in the Tower that she could neither hear of their health nor receive any direction from them'.[19]

Although conditions were bad and Blood's health may have suffered, his spirit was undaunted. Most people in his situation as they sat in a dark dungeon would begin to contemplate how their life was about to end on the gallows. However, as tales of his infamy spread ever further throughout the land, Blood, when questioned by the Provost Marshal, Sir Gilbert Talbot, and the magistrates, Sir William Waller and Dr Chamberlain, announced arrogantly that he would confess to no one but the King. This intrepid survivor had not yet dealt his final hand.

12

'THE MERRY MONARCH'

The most notorious outlaw of his day had demanded an audience with the King and Charles had agreed to meet him. Most people were bemused at this, as they believed that Blood had no hope of receiving a royal pardon. Was he not the man who had been involved in a multitude of plots against the King? Had he not attempted to abduct and murder the Duke of Ormonde on the streets of London? The authorities had been trying to capture him for years and now he had stolen the King's own crown from under their noses at the Tower of London. Subsequent developments can only be understood if we consider the character of the King with whom Blood was about to meet.

When King Charles I had been blessed with a son on 29 May 1630, hope and joy were felt throughout the nation. In June the young prince was christened Charles by William Laud, then Bishop of London, at a lavish ceremony in the private chapel of St James's Palace, for which the holy water was brought from the River Jordan.[1] His early childhood was a happy one, spent in pleasant surroundings, with plenty of time to play with his siblings and the Villiers children, and a fitting education. All seemed well for his future.

The Queen's Roman Catholic influence on the young prince was of grave concern to Protestants from the

Colonel Blood, the man who stole the Crown Jewels from the Tower of
London, by G. White. (*By courtesy of the National Library of Ireland*)

King Charles II pictured with his regalia, by John Michael Wright.
(*The Royal Collection © Her Majesty Queen Elizabeth II*)

James Butler (1610–88), 1st Duke of Ormonde. Blood was his bitter enemy and attempted to kidnap and murder him in London. (*By courtesy of the National Portrait Gallery, London*)

George Villiers (1628–87), 2nd Duke of Buckingham, by Sir Peter Lely. Buckingham was believed to have been at the back of a number of Blood's daring adventures. (*By courtesy of the National Portrait Gallery, London*)

The Tower of London in 1660. Engraving by Wenceslaus Hollar.
(*The Stapleton Collection/ Bridgeman Art Gallery*)

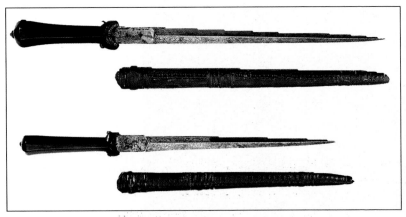

The longer dagger and sheath are believed to be those used by Blood in his theft of the Crown Jewels and taken from him when he was captured. They are at present in the possession of the Royal Armouries at the Tower of London. The shorter weapon and sheath are believed to have been taken from his accomplice Perrott. (© *The Board of Trustees of the Armouries*)

The upper part of the Martin Tower at the Tower of London, where Talbot Edwards and his family lived, as it is today.
(*David C. Hanrahan*)

The lower part of the Martin Tower, from where Blood stole the Crown Jewels.
(*David C. Hanrahan*)

Blood and his gang make off with the Crown Jewels while Talbot Edwards lies injured on the ground. (*By courtesy of the National Library of Ireland*)

Blood & his Accomplices *making their* Escape *after* Stealing *the* Crown *from the* TOWER *of* LONDON.

Colonel Blood told Charles II that he had once been ready to assassinate His Majesty as he bathed in the river and was only prevented at the last moment by the feelings of awe he experienced on seeing the King. (*Mary Evans Picture Library*)

Letter sent by Thomas Blood to the Duke of Ormonde apologising for his attack on him. The writing of this letter is believed to have been one of the conditions of Blood's lenient treatment by King Charles II after the theft of the Crown Jewels. (*MS. Carte 69, folio 164r, The Bodleian Library, University of Oxford*)

Visitors to the Crown Jewel Room in the nineteenth century.
(*Mary Evans Picture Library*)

The display of the Crown Jewels at the Tower of London in modern times.
Security is much tighter now than in Blood's day!
(*Crown © Historic Royal Palaces*)

beginning. One cause of discontent were the visits being paid by the prince to his mother's chapel, where he was said to have attended the Roman Catholic mass.[2] This was a practice the King was forced to put a stop to. Charles I also insisted that his son give back the 'sacred medals and crucifixes' that he had won from his mother while playing parlour games.[3]

Of those who influenced Charles as a child the most significant was probably the Duke of Newcastle, who was appointed as his governor. It was he who introduced Charles to the delights of activities such as riding, fencing and dancing, as well as imparting a philosophy of life founded on good relations with people. He told the young boy: 'sometimes . . . a smile in the right place will advantage you'.[4]

Life was not to run smoothly for this young prince. Charles's idyllic lifestyle was brought crashing down with the outbreak of the Civil War and the execution of his father. The young prince was thrown into an uncertain world and became a king in exile of a divided nation at the age of eighteen. He had to live under difficult conditions, subject to the good will of various monarchs around Europe, 'as poor as the mice behind the wainscotting of his little chapel'.[5]

During this time he brokered a deal with the Scottish Presbyterians under which, in return for concessions, he became their king. His acceptance of the Covenants was more of an exercise in expediency than sincerity, his ultimate aim being the invasion and recapture of England.[6] His coronation took place in Scotland in 1651. When the Cromwellian armies invaded Scotland he led an army into England. However, when Cromwell caught up with him at Worcester he was forced to flee. The story of the young royal's escape using various disguises, including that of a labourer, and taking refuge in the humble houses of commoners to evade the Cromwellians, has gained mythic proportions over the years. He was forced back into exile on the continent once again.

These years in exile gave Charles many experiences that are usually denied to someone of his standing. From hard times an interesting character developed. There was undoubtedly a strong element of the rogue in Charles, which exhibited itself in his pursuit of adventure, excitement and pleasure. The Merry Monarch, as he became known, enjoyed a good story just as much as he did music, dancing and fine food. During his time in exile in France he liked to play billiards and swim.[7] While at Spa in 1654 Charles and his court 'spent the days drinking spring water and hunting in the nearby hills and the evenings singing, dancing, and drinking Rhenish wine'.[8]

Although a Protestant visitor to Charles II's court at Flanders in the 1650s stated that religious services were held twice daily in the royal presence, it seems that this was not the full story, as a Cromwellian spy noted the drunkenness, fornication and adultery there.[9] Ormonde, around the same time, complained of the King's 'immoderate delight in empty, effeminate and vulgar conversations'.[10] There is also evidence of his many frivolous interests at the time, including the possession of a pet monkey, having a camel transported to his court, the presence of French comedians, harpers and fiddlers, and his losses at gambling.[11]

Charles also had a strong interest in the theatre. It was an interest that he brought back to England with him after the Restoration, when as King he insisted that any theatres licensed by him would dispense with the old practice of having female parts played by boys and instead use women. This was just one of the many conventions he brought back with him from France, along with a liking for French tutors, and 'long wigs, face-paint, muffs and perfume' for men.[12]

He always possessed a great enthusiasm for riding and hunting. In 1665 he instituted a race to be held at Newmarket every year. The race was four miles long on grass and Charles's novel method of spectating was to wait for the competitors half-way along the course and then follow them at full gallop to the finishing line.[13] He also enjoyed activities such as fishing, and playing games like pall-mall[14] and 'real' tennis.

Nowhere was this interest in the pursuit of pleasure more notable than in his dealings with women. Even at a young age this trait had begun to assert itself when he was said to have been interested in the 'licentious conversation of the debauched soldiers', a fact that did not please Clarendon.[15] Throughout his life he had relationships with a variety of women and fathered numerous bastards. He was only eighteen when, during his time in exile, he fell in love with Lucy Walter and she gave birth to his first son. Later, Lucy's actions were said to be causing embarrassment when it became known that she had had an affair with a married man, Thomas Howard, at The Hague. She was also being blackmailed by her maid, who claimed that Lucy had induced two abortions on herself. She told an agent, who had been sent to her on behalf of Charles, that she intended to kill the maid using a knitting needle![16] By 1657, however, Lucy's relationship with Howard had gone awry and she persuaded a cousin to murder him on a visit to Brussels. As it happened, he survived the attack but was wounded. She then began to hint that she might publish Charles's letters to her if she did not receive money from him. This, along with her poor performance as a mother, convinced Charles that his son was best removed from her. When this was attempted she managed to avoid it by running into the street, screaming loudly. Charles did finally manage to get custody of the boy in 1658, whereupon he sent him to Paris. Soon afterwards Lucy died of venereal disease. The boy was later to become the Duke of Monmouth and a contender for the throne.[17]

While in exile in France, Charles had an affair with Elizabeth Killigrew, and perhaps also with Lord Byron's widow Eleanor and with the duchesse de Châtillon.[18] There was also an affair with Catherine Pegge, the daughter of a Derbyshire gentleman, which took place during his time at

Flanders in the 1650s. Catherine gave birth to a son and a daughter. The son, Charles Fitzcharles, was acknowledged by the King when he arrived in London some fourteen years later.[19]

One of the most precious and enduring relationships of his life was that with his long-term mistress Barbara Villiers, wife of the Earl of Castlemaine, Roger Palmer, and cousin of Buckingham. Even though their relationship caused considerable scandal at various times during his reign, Charles refused to relent. When he first met Barbara she was described as 'a ravishing nineteen-year-old . . . with auburn hair, deep blue eyes, and a nature passionate in and out of the bedchamber'.[20]

Even when his new queen, Catherine of Braganza, arrived from Portugal Barbara was already pregnant with their second child. The new queen was very different in character from Barbara, having been reared in a convent. To make matters more difficult for her, she spoke no English on her arrival. Soon after the baby was born and given the name Charles at a public christening ceremony, Barbara left her husband and the King agreed to appoint her Lady of the Queen's Bedchamber. When the Queen became aware of what was going on she was not pleased. Clarendon had also tried to object to the affair but was met with a firm rebuttal in the form of a letter from Charles in which he wrote '. . . I am resolved to go through with this matter, let what will come of it'.[21]

Charles would spend several nights a week at Barbara's lodgings in the Palace and could often be seen making his way back across the garden early in the morning.[22] The Queen's lack of influence on the issue was amply demonstrated at a party held at Somerset House in September 1662 when Charles arrived accompanied by his Queen, Barbara Villiers and his son by Lucy Walter. After the party 'husband and wife, mistress and former mistress's son, went home affectionately together in the same coach'.[23]

By the middle of the 1660s Barbara had given birth to five of Charles's children.[24] With the passing of years the passion he felt for Barbara might have waned but he never deserted her. In 1668, when their love affair was effectively over, he bought her Berkshire House and in 1670 created her Duchess of Cleveland. At one point Barbara converted to Roman Catholicism and Charles was urged by her relatives to change her mind; he just told them 'as for the souls of the ladies, he never meddled there'.[25]

Charles also fell in love with that other beautiful woman at his court, the very attractive Frances Stuart, or, as she was known, *la belle* Stuart. Frances, who had been forced into exile with her family during the Civil War and educated in France, was sent over to Charles's court by his sister, Henrietta, to be maid of honour to the Queen. It seems that Charles's love for Frances never became physical, not through his lack of desire but purely because of her resolve. His deep affection for her is shown by the poetry he wrote about his love for her and by the fact that he used her image as the profile of Britannia on his coinage.[26] When Frances ran off and married the Duke of Richmond and Lennox, Charles was so upset that he vowed never to see her again. However, when she became ill with smallpox he changed his mind, decided to forgive her and went to her sickbed. She recovered and they were to remain close friends for the rest of his life.

Undoubtedly Charles's interest in the stage led him to have relationships with the actresses Moll Davies and Nell Gwynne. As a result of their relatively short dalliance, Moll gave birth to his daughter, while Nell, the 'bold, merry slut', as Pepys called her, gave birth to his son in 1670 and a second shortly afterwards.[27]

Then there was Louise de Kéroüalle, who came over from France, where she had had a post in waiting to Charles's sister Henrietta. When her mistress died she was sent over to England to work for the Queen. It was not long before Charles began to seduce her, aided in this endeavour by Lord Arlington. Although Louise was not all that enamoured of the idea she eventually gave in to his pressure. Nine months after their first 'encounter' at Arlington's mansion she gave birth to a son. She became renowned for her expensive tastes, which Charles did his best to satisfy.[28] She is estimated to have cost the nation about £40,000 a year in pension and presents.[29] On one occasion he made her ill by passing on a venereal disease to her and gave her jewellery to the value of £10,000 as a token of his sorrow.[30] As a sign of his affection he bestowed on her the title Duchess of Portsmouth.

Hortense Mancini, the Duchess of Mazarin, another mistress of Charles's, became a fierce rival of Louise's. It is revealing that once Charles fell for Hortense he urged Louise to get an allowance from her husband![31] Hortense was a niece of the Italian Cardinal Jules Mazarin, who had been chief minister of France. She was thirty years of age when she first met Charles and he was immediately captured by her beauty, her 'full smooth features, jet black hair, and eyes that changed colour with the light'.[32] Her personality would also have made her attractive to him; she was confident and liked to 'gamble, eat, shoot, and swim, and was noted for her trick of performing a Spanish dance while accompanying herself on a guitar'.[33]

In the midst of all these illicit relationships and illegitimate children the Queen remained childless. This was a worry to all concerned with maintaining the Protestant monarchy, since Charles's brother, James, was a Roman Catholic. The Queen tried various remedies, including the healing waters at Tunbridge Wells and Bath, but still no successful pregnancy resulted. She suffered a number of miscarriages through the years, including one which was allegedly caused by the King's pet fox jumping on to her bed.[34] There was widespread concern when in October of 1663 she fell seriously ill and almost died.

Charles was kind to his queen and resolutely refused to divorce her. However, his infidelity did affect her. From

1674 she began to spend her summers separated from him and the unhappiness she felt about their marriage was demonstrated when she publicly berated Charles at Windsor in 1683 for humiliating her. On another occasion she cried openly when Louise decided it would be funny for her as the King's mistress to wait upon the Queen's table with the other servants.[35]

Charles's reputation as the idle, fun-loving, woman-chasing monarch is well established, yet there were other sides to his character. In spite of his reputation as an idler he could be hard working. He was forced to operate under a highly centralised system of government, which meant that at times he was weighed down with work. He would rise most mornings at five or six and was a regular attender of the Privy Council, the Foreign Affairs Committee and the House of Lords.[36] Although he was punctual in his attendance at meetings and often contributed to debates, he disliked reading and writing and preferred having things read aloud to him.[37]

Although not renowned as an intellectual, there was a strong inquisitive and intellectual aspect to his character.[38] He had a wide range of interests and a special fascination for the unusual or novel. Evelyn, the diarist, writes about his having discussed with Charles subjects as diverse as 'shipping, architecture, bee-keeping, gardening, and urban pollution'.[39]

Charles's great interest in all things to do with science, invention and exploration was well known. He pursued his interest in alchemy with the Duke of Buckingham while in exile, became the first patron of the Royal Society and frequently showed his enthusiasm for their activities. Unfortunately the King's opinion of a promise made by Buckingham to bring the society a piece of unicorn's horn is not documented.[40] Charles's interest in scientific matters was demonstrated on one occasion when he expressed a desire for 'a lunar globe, with the hills, eminences and cavities of the moon's surfaces as well as the degree of whiteness solidly moulded'.[41] At Whitehall he had his own private room in which he kept all his clocks, maps, model ships and other such things. He was known for setting his watch religiously every morning by the sundial in the garden. In his bedroom he was said to have had seven clocks, which annoyed the servants by chiming at different times![42]

He was also a devoted lover of ships and all maritime matters. His love of science and the sea combined in his interest in the problem of ships determining their position accurately at sea. Louise de Kéroüalle, knowing of his interest, introduced him to a Frenchman who had devised a solution to the problem based on the position of the moon and certain stars. The King had the idea investigated by a number of experts who reported that the theory was problematic in view of the absence of any good star maps or known route for the moon. The King responded by setting up the Observatory at Greenwich and appointing John Flamsteed as his first Astronomical Observator, later known as the Astronomer Royal. It was a work Flamsteed was to be engaged in for more than forty years and resulted in his posthumously published star catalogue in 1725.[43]

The King's strong interest and belief in astrology was demonstrated by his annoyance when he discovered that Buckingham had retained Dr Heydon to cast his horoscope. There was also an occasion during Charles's exile in Paris when an astrologer had, it seems, predicted both his restoration and his celebrated entry into London on 29 May 1660. He held the man's abilities in high regard and in 1678 he ordered the English ambassador in Paris, Montague, to consult him again to hear his predictions for the future. This time it brought about complications when it was claimed that Montague had pursued the rather treacherous plan of getting the man to predict whatever he ordered him to. This claim was made by Barbara Villiers, who had been having a relationship with Montague. When they quarrelled she decided to inform the King of his ambassador's roguery![44]

Charles is often thought of as a lightweight in the political arena. But his unique background, being forced to survive in very difficult conditions during the Civil War and after, had made him a pragmatist with very astute political skills. As one writer describes him, he was 'not a carefree playboy but a hard-bitten politician: wily, manipulative and cynical, a survivor in a dangerous world'.[45] He was capable of looking at a situation and working out the most favourable course of action for himself. The pragmatic and cynical side to his nature is shown by his involvement with the two Treaties of Dover. This political dexterity is the trait that he would employ when faced with Blood.

He was also known to have a forgiving nature, which was probably another aspect of his pragmatic side. One day he announced that he was prepared to forgive anyone in the country except for the horse that had thrown him in the morning![46] A remarkable measure of his capacity for forgiveness is the fact that ten years after the Restoration he was willing to visit Cromwell's son Henry at his house near Newmarket.[47] Then there is the case of William Petty, who worked for the Commonwealth when he compiled his Survey of Ireland. Petty attempted to apologise and explain his actions to the King. Charles simply replied, 'But, Doctor, why have you left off your inquiries into the mechanics of shipping?'[48]

There was thus great interest in how the King would interact with the notorious Colonel Blood.

13

IT WAS FOR A CROWN

Blood defiantly commented to Captain Beckman after his capture that 'It was a gallant attempt, though unsuccessful, for it was for a crown'.[1] In the aftermath of this 'gallant attempt' upon the Crown Jewels the name Colonel Blood was spoken of everywhere. In coffee houses and inns, where people spoke of little else but his outrageous and daring attempt to steal the Crown Jewels from the Tower of London, Blood's already considerable notoriety was increased. Balladeers sang of his deeds and newsletters gave full accounts of this assault on the symbol of royal authority, the Crown Jewels.

Even poets were inspired to write on the adventure. Take for instance this by Andrew Marvell:

Epigramme Upon Blood's attempt to steale the Crown

> When daring *Blood*, his rents to have regain'd,
> Upon the *English* Diadem distrain'd,
> He chose the Cassok, surcingle, and Gown
> (No mask so fit for one that robbs a Crown);
> But his lay-pity underneath prevayl'd
> And while he spar'd the *Keeper's* life, he fail'd.
> With the Priests Vestments had he but put on
> A Bishops cruelty, the Crown was gone.[2]

News of Blood's infamy did not fail to reach the country of his birth, as shown by the following correspondence from Robert Leigh in Dublin, writing to Secretary Williamson at the time. Sure that Blood would finally get the punishment he was due, he wrote:

Little news since my last except that of the bold attempt of that notorious villain, Thomas Blood, upon the crown, which makes all honest men rejoice that he is at last taken, as well in hopes that he will discover some of his traitors and those that attempted to murder the Duke of Ormonde, as that he will receive the reward of his many wicked attempts, both here and in England . . .[3]

Although the Crown Jewels had survived this determined attempt to steal them, the incident was not without cost. The sceptre had been damaged by the file of Thomas Blood junior and the State Crown had been disfigured so badly by the mallet blows of his father that the King had to have a new one made at a cost of £7,870.[4] Even though an apprentice barber is reported to have returned a diamond he had found, and a 'poor Sinder-woman' a pearl, several of the precious stones were never seen again.[5]

Although it had been widely believed that Blood's request for an audience with the King would be turned down, on 12 May 1671 this belief was shown to be false. The state papers note the meeting between Blood and Charles II as follows: 'Old Blood was on the 12th brought from the Tower to Court, where he was privately examined by his Majesty . . .'.[6]

It was a development that disturbed Ormonde greatly when he became aware of it, and caused him to state prophetically that 'surely no king should wish to see a malefactor, but with intention to pardon him'.[7] Once face to face with the King, Blood confessed to the 1663 plot to take Dublin Castle, the escape of Mason and the attempted kidnapping of the Duke of Ormonde in London, giving as motivation the fact that the Duke had been responsible for the confiscation of his lands in Ireland and the killing of some of his friends. It was said that he refused to name any of his accomplices in these deeds, even to the King.

He then went on to inform Charles impertinently that he had once been given the assignment of killing His Majesty. The plan was that he should lie hidden in the reeds of the Thames at a place in Battersea Park where the King was in the habit of bathing, and from there he was to shoot him. Blood had taken up his position as planned but, he explained, once he laid eyes on the King he was so awestruck by the sight of royalty that he could not carry out the deed and in fact persuaded his accomplices to desist from the plan altogether.

He then attempted to persuade the King that to have him executed would be a serious mistake, since hundreds of his friends were sworn to avenge his death and this would create a very dangerous situation for His Majesty. On the other hand, he claimed, if he were spared he would become a loyal subject.

At the end of the audience Blood was sent back once again to the Tower. In July, much to the surprise of a great many people, Lord Arlington issued warrants for the release of both Blood and Perrott. Sir John Robinson informed Williamson of the development in the following manner: 'Lord Arlington dined with me at the Tower on Saturday, and gave me the warrants for the release of old Blood and Perrott, and for the confinement of young Blood, which is accordingly done . . .'[8]

Furthermore, on 1 August 1671 Blood was officially pardoned for all his crimes: 'Grant of pardon to Thomas Blood, the father, of all treasons, murders, felonies, &c., committed by him alone, or together with others from 29 May 1660.'[9]

On 31 August Thomas Blood junior was released and both he and Perrott were also given pardons. For those who were scandalised by these acts of extreme royal leniency, insult was added to injury when all Blood's lands in Ireland, which were worth £500 a year, were restored to him. He did experience some difficulty in removing them from the grasp of Toby Barnes, who fought him in the courts. The term for which Barnes had been leased the land had not expired and Blood was forced to get the King to authorise the Lord Lieutenant to issue a licence to enable him to bring a writ of error for reversing his outlawry before he could finally take possession.[10]

This incredible turn of events by which Blood found himself restored to freedom and wealth seems even more surprising when compared to the treatment Edwards received. The poor man received a grant of £200 for himself and £100 for his son, but the payment was so slow in coming that he was forced to sell the orders for it at a discount of 50 per cent in order to pay his medical expenses! He died shortly afterwards on 30 September 1674. His tombstone can be seen in the south wall of the Chapel of St Peter ad Vincula within the Tower of London.[11]

One rather bizarre condition of Blood's release was that he should write an abject letter of apology to Ormonde for his part in the attack on him and ask for his pardon. He did so in the following words:

My Lord,
The greatnesse of my Crimes soe farr exceeds expression that weare not my burdened soule incuraged by findin vent to its griefe, though by such an acknowledgement as beares little proportion to my guilt, I had forborne this further trouble to Your Grace, but overcharg'd with increasing sorrow by the consideration of your renowned excellency which, I unworthy monster was soe regardles off, hath produced this erruption of the humble acknowledgement of my most hainous Crime, for which as I have a deepe impression of hart

Compunction, soe should I count it my happiness to have an opportunity in the most demonstrative waye to manifest it Your Grace, who am unworthy to be accounted, though, in reality, I am
Your Graces most humble Servant,
Tho. Blood[12]

The King also sent the Duke a letter outlining his reasons for his actions, now lost. Lord Arlington also worked very hard to bring about a peace between Blood and Ormonde. Publicly, Ormonde felt that he had no option but to accept the situation, saying, 'If the King could forgive an attempt on his crown, I myself may easily forgive an attempt on my life, and since it is his Majesty's pleasure, that is reason sufficient for me.' However, that Ormonde's personal feelings were probably quite different can be gleaned from the fact that whenever he came eye to eye with Blood in the years that followed, as he did quite frequently at court, he resolutely ignored him.

An interesting aside to all this is a letter that the King received in May, reputedly from Blood while still in captivity at the Tower, in which it was claimed that two important figures, Sir Thomas Osborne and Sir Thomas Littleton, were behind his attempt on the Crown:

May it please your Majestie, these may tell and inform you, that it was Sir Thomas Osborn and Sir Thomas Littleton, both your tresurers for your Navey, that sett me to steall your crowne, but he that feed me with money was James Littleton, Esquire. 'Tis he that pays under the tresurers at your pay office. He is a very bold villainous fellow, a very rogue, for I and my companions have had a 100l. of hime of youer Majestie's money to incurag us upon this attempt. I pray noe words of this conffession, but know your friends. Nott else, but am youre Majestie's prisoner, and if life spared youer dutifull subjectt whose name is Blood, which I hope is not that your Majestie seeks after.[13]

In reality this letter proved to be nothing more than an attempt by an enemy of Osborne and Littleton to implicate those two gentlemen in the greatest crime of the age. The letter is obviously not in Blood's handwriting and is in fact believed to be a rather imaginative forgery![14]

The question has often been asked why the amazing decision was made by the King to release and in effect reward such a notorious outlaw as Thomas Blood. It was no less a cause for surprise at the time. The diarist Evelyn wrote of meeting Blood shortly after the pardon in this manner:

How he ever came to be pardoned and ever received into favour, not only after this but several other exploits almost as daring, both in Ireland and here, I never could come to understand. This man had not only a daring, but a villainous unmerciful look, a false countenance, but very well spoken, and dangerously insinuating.

A number of explanations for Charles's incredible leniency have been proposed. One very unlikely view is that it was Charles himself who had put Blood up to stealing the Crown Jewels in the hope that they could be used to raise much-needed revenue. One fact often alluded to is that Blood managed to make a favourable impression upon the King with, as one writer puts it, 'his daring, his effrontery and his adventures'.[15] A contemporary tells us that Blood 'answered so frankly and undauntedly that everyone stood amazed'.[16] The argument goes that the King was so struck by Blood's personality that he decided to grant him a pardon on that basis alone. A favourable response from the King towards a character such as Blood would not be out of character for the Merry Monarch;

after all, had he not always found Buckingham similarly intriguing? There was undoubtedly a strong element in the King's character that caused him to admire an adventurous character like Blood, and indeed curiosity probably influenced him when he decided to meet this daring fellow in the first place. However, it is too simplistic to argue that Charles pardoned Blood purely because he had 'a fellow feeling for the insane daring'[17] of the man.

If it were true, as many believed, that Blood was working on behalf of Buckingham, the Duke would have used any influence at his disposal to have his man pardoned. We know that some influential people who were part of Buckingham's group did speak in support of Blood. For example there was Prince Rupert, the King's cousin, who we know described Blood at the time as having been once a 'very stout, bold fellow in the royal service'. And then there was Barbara Villiers, whose role as an advocate of Blood's could also have been significant.

Most important of all must have been the influence of the King's intelligence people, namely Lord Arlington, who was Secretary of State, and his Under-Secretary, Sir Joseph Williamson. Some even suspect that Blood may have been on the government's payroll from a much earlier period.[18] There is little doubt that these 'spy-masters' regarded Blood as a 'catch' of immense value to them. In fact, Joseph Williamson himself stated the matter quite clearly in 1671 when he wrote, 'God has made us Masters of Blood [and] it is often times ye value . . . of the Crowne itself.'[19] As one writer puts it: 'Here was a man with an almost unrivalled knowledge of the radical community in all three kingdoms and the Netherlands, and with a reputation as a fearless opponent of the regime.'[20] Considering this perception of Blood's value, Arlington and Williamson would surely have had an influence on the King's final decision, although

Williamson would have preferred the whole thing to have been arranged in private. He wrote in 1671: 'Better Blood had not come to the King openly, but privately. The phanaticks will not believe one that comes to Court, though it were an angel.'[21]

It would have been a terrible waste from the perspective of people like Arlington and Williamson to execute someone so potentially valuable. Arlington's efforts at bringing about a reconciliation between Blood and Ormonde also suggest how heavily involved he was in obtaining Blood's pardon.

Blood had no doubt banked on this from the beginning. After all, it was he who had demanded to see the King. He was not in any way reticent about extolling his own virtues to the regime. When the King reputedly asked him the question 'What if I should give you your life?', Blood's reply was a pointed: 'I would endeavour to deserve it.'[22] He knew that he was in a dire situation and he was prepared to use whatever he had to bargain for his life.

The prevailing political situation undoubtedly strengthened Blood's bargaining position. A new war with Holland was brewing and Charles felt it imperative to ensure that these troublesome 'phanaticks' at home would not ally themselves with the Dutch. He wanted to pacify these potential rebels before confronting the foreign enemy. As a move towards achieving this he was at this stage planning to face down opposition from within Parliament and take the courageous step of issuing an indulgence to both Roman Catholics and Protestant Nonconformists. Now luck had presented him with Blood, a man of significant symbolic value within the Nonconformist community, with an unequalled reputation and an unsurpassed knowledge of his co-religionists' identities and activities. Blood's value to the regime would be as an intermediary between the King and his Nonconformist enemies, and also as an informant. Blood's political background made him invaluable to Charles,

Arlington and Williamson. Blood possessed what they needed and they possessed Blood's life.

The truth behind the pardoning of Blood was that it constituted part of a political strategy. It was not the Charles of mythology, the Merry Monarch, the lover of fun and excitement who pardoned the notorious Thomas Blood. The King was not some sort of fool who was sufficiently impressed by the audacity and daring of his prisoner to pardon him. He was above all a pragmatist. It was Charles the cunning politician who made this decision. Blood was regarded as a tool for the use of his regime. Charles spoke to Blood, calculated how useful he could be in the implementation of his planned policies towards the Nonconformists, negotiations were conducted and a deal was struck.

Blood was too cunning to make the negotiations easy for the King and by September the terms of his pardon were still being argued over. Two peers, Lord Holles and Lord Ashley, had a number of meetings with him in order to settle the issue. At one point in the negotiations it appears that Blood was pushing for the governorship of a plantation, probably in America, but the regime wanted him much nearer to home than that. In the end he settled for financial rewards at home, or as Williamson's notes put it, 'that the King would provide for him'.[23]

For his part, the fact that promises were made by Blood regarding his assistance to the regime is underlined in a letter written by Sir John Robinson to Williamson on 23 December 1671 wherein he states: 'Mr. Blood sometimes visits me, and tells me he has been faithful in keeping his promises.'[24]

Meanwhile, as the general public was not privy to any deals or negotiations, people were shocked by the pardon of a renowned troublemaker like Blood. Widespread popular surprise and disbelief at Blood's pardon is best captured by these lines from a satirical verse entitled 'The Chronicle', sometimes attributed, perhaps incorrectly, to the pen of Lord Rochester:

IT WAS FOR A CROWN

Blood, that wears treason in his face,
Villain complete in parson's gown,
How much is he at court in grace
For stealing Ormond and the crown!
Since loyalty does no man good,
Let's steal the King and outdo Blood.[25]

14

SEVENTEENTH-CENTURY ESPIONAGE

How a notorious criminal like Blood came to be treated in such a lenient manner by the King is not the only aspect of his life to raise questions. There is one accusation against him that, above all others, has continued to circulate and to demand attention. This is the suspicion that during his time on the run in the 1660s Blood was not really a fugitive at all, but was in fact an informer on the payroll of the King. This, it is claimed, is why it appeared that he had evaded arrest so successfully during this period. The claim is also used to explain the King's favourable treatment of him after his theft of the Crown Jewels.

It is well documented that there was a very active world of government-sponsored espionage in existence during this period.[1] The centre of this world was to be found in the office of the Secretaries of State, of which there were two, the Northern and the Southern. Between 1662 and 1674 the most dominant of these Secretaries was in the Southern Office. He was the talented Sir Henry Bennet, Earl of Arlington, who spoke Latin, French and Spanish fluently but could be somewhat pompous and foppish, a side of his nature that left him open to the satire of his enemy the Duke of Buckingham. A bad scar meant that Lord Arlington always wore a black patch on one eye.[2] The fact that he was married to Lady Ossory's sister made Buckingham like him all the less. However, the length of time that he spent as Secretary of State testifies to the esteem in which Charles II held him. He was not above taking on the duty of persuading women such as Frances Stuart and Louise de Kéroüalle into becoming the King's mistress.[3]

The main responsibility for the practical direction of espionage activities within Arlington's office fell to his Under-Secretary, Sir Joseph Williamson. Williamson's responsibilities included the training and placing of agents in the field, maintaining contact with them and organising their payments. He was in effect the human link between Arlington and the agents. Although Arlington grew to trust Williamson implicitly and delegated much of the day-to-day running of the Office to him, their relationship had not begun so amicably. In fact one of Arlington's first acts on being appointed was to dismiss Williamson from his post.

Born in 1633, Williamson was the son of a Cumberland vicar and had no financial means to speak of when he went to London in the late 1640s as clerk and amanuensis to his local MP, Richard Tolson. However, Tolson supported his education at Westminster School and Queen's College, Oxford, where he graduated with a Bachelor of Arts degree followed later by a Master's degree and a Fellowship. In fact, had he not been tempted by ambitions of higher power he may well have pursued an academic life. But at the age of twenty-seven, assisted by the Bishop of London, Gilbert Sheldon, he managed to obtain a position as clerk to the then Secretary of State, Sir Edward Nicholas. Although Arlington dismissed him when he became Secretary of State in 1662 he soon realised how pivotal Williamson was to the running of the Office and quickly reinstated him.[4] Williamson was also notable for his social talents. It was said that he was able to 'dance six hours at a stretch, play musical instruments, and perform juggling acts'.[5] A bond of trust soon developed between Arlington and Williamson and they became a very effective and successful team.

A most important area of operations in the information-gathering business was the Post Office.[6] Arlington held the position of Postmaster General from 1667 but even before that Williamson was directing many covert operations there. At the General Letter Office correspondence was targeted, intercepted and copied if necessary, while ciphers were decoded and languages translated. Mathematicians, cipher experts and linguists were all in place to undertake this important work. Even in 1666, in an attempt to capture Blood and his fellow rebels, Williamson was having mail intercepted that he believed was on its way to them. In a memorandum headed 'Mene Tekel, Blood, Alexander, &c' he wrote: '. . . intercept all letters coming from Ireland addressed to John Knipe, Aldersgate Street, or letters going to Ireland, addressed to Dan. Edgerton, Cook Street, Dublin'.[7]

The Post Office was also used for the transfer of written reports from his agents in the field to Williamson. This was done by the use of code names and addresses of which certain staff in the General Letter Office were aware. Williamson supplied them with the list and they knew that any correspondence addressed to persons on it was for his eyes alone. Although the list is now lost, its entries may be similar to those found in his personal address book, which dates from 1663 to 1667 and contains the real names of many of his agents, as well as their code names.[8] Another important source of information was the interrogation of prisoners, which was often carried out by Arlington or Williamson themselves. Indeed, even Charles was not averse to carrying out an interrogation personally.[9]

In many cases prisoners were 'turned', drafted on to the payroll and sent back into the field as government agents. Their escape would be arranged and they would be sent out among their peers to begin their work for Williamson. The case of William Leving is an example of this and shows how precarious and difficult the life of an informer was.[10] After his arrest for his part in a plot in Durham in 1663 there was ample evidence to hang Leving, so he began to impart information to his captors in order to save his life. He even gave accounts of the conversations he heard taking place between his fellow prisoners. Leving's escape was soon engineered and he began relaying information back to the authorities under his code name, 'Leonard Williams'.

Leving was responsible for exposing a plot being planned for London in the 1660s. He managed to ingratiate himself with a gang, which included Mason and Blood, that intended to take the Tower of London and attack Whitehall Palace. Leving refers in his information to a Mr Allen, but on the document someone has written 'his true name is Bludd' above this name.[11]

It was eventually decided to arrest one member of the gang called John Atkinson, alias Dr Johnson. Although Leving supplied his employers with the time and place to catch this man they arrived too early and discovered another man, Richardson, alias Fawcett, there instead. Much to Leving's annoyance they did not arrest Richardson and he warned Atkinson and all the others. Luckily for him, Leving was not suspected by the other members of the gang, and was himself also warned by them!

Eventually, however, suspicion did fall on Leving because of the interference of another government agent called Henry North. North became involved with the same rebel group, but when they began to suspect him he named Leving as the informer. Although he had to endure a robust questioning at the end of a pistol, Leving skilfully managed to talk his way out of the situation by throwing the guilt back on North. Shortly afterwards, and with Leving's assistance, Atkinson was arrested by the authorities. Arlington took part in the interrogation, by means of which the names were discovered of some members of the group, including that of Blood.[12]

By April of 1665 Leving felt that he was in a very dangerous position and asked for permission to leave London for a while, which he was granted. However, he soon found himself back in the capital and struggling to survive on very little money. Leving's situation was alleviated when he and another agent called William Freer did some work in Ireland for Arlington, with the permission of Ormonde, for over two months in 1666.

Back in England once again, Leving got drawn into the controversy surrounding the warrant for the arrest of the Duke of Buckingham for his association with Dr John Heydon the astrologer. Leving and Freer were among those who made statements implicating Buckingham in the affair. However, as noted, Buckingham escaped arrest and eventually managed to ingratiate himself once again with the King.

In early 1667 Leving applied to Williamson for a warrant to apprehend Blood and a number of other wanted people, including Lockyer and Butler. The warrants were drawn up at Whitehall in March 1667:

> Warrants from Lord Arlington to Leonard Williams, alias Wm. Leving, to search for Major Blood, Timothy Butler, Capt. Lockyer . . . to seize them, and any instruments of war that may be in the places where they are seized, and bring them before him, if taken in London or Westminster, or, if in the country, before the nearest deputy lieutenant or justice of peace.[13]

Of course he failed to arrest Blood.

Financial difficulties led to Leving and Freer taking up highway robbery around the north of England, where Leving was soon arrested. Thus it happened that he was being transported as a prisoner from Newgate when Blood, Lockyer and Butler set upon the party to free their friend Mason in 1667. Leving was being brought to York reluctantly to act as a crown witness against John Atkinson and some other rebels for their part in the plot of 1663. No wonder he was afraid of what Blood and the others would do to him if given the opportunity. Not long after the Mason escape he was found dead in his prison cell, most probably poisoned. His friend Freer was in no doubt that Leving had been murdered when he expressed his fear to Williamson about being sent to York Castle because of 'his being in danger of being poisoned by the same that did it to Mr. Leving'.[14] Leving's murder could have been the revenge of either Blood or Buckingham or perhaps both.

Apart from his spies and informers, Williamson also had information coming to him from a network of local officials, ranging from Lords Lieutenant to Justices of the Peace, who corresponded with him regularly and kept him informed of local dissenters, plotters and general troublemakers.[15]

With the departure of Arlington in 1674 Williamson himself became Secretary of State, having paid his old boss £6,000 for the privilege. However, without Arlington the influence of the Office began to dwindle. Things did not go well personally for Williamson when he was damaged by the repercussions of the Popish Plot and eventually removed from office in 1679.[16]

We know that after his pardon for the theft of the Crown Jewels Blood became an invaluable part of the government machinery and had regular dealings with Williamson during this time. However, the accusation has been levelled against him that prior to his arrest in 1671 Blood was already working as a secret agent employed by Arlington and Williamson. Evidence has been offered to support this contention.

Until recently one strong piece of evidence in support of this claim was the existence of certain government letters which concern the release of a man from gaol on Blood's endorsement in the year 1666. The argument questions how Blood could have endorsed the release of a man from gaol in the 1660s if he was himself an outlaw on the run. If this were true he would undoubtedly have been on the government payroll. However, it has been shown that these documents are misdated in the records and in fact date from 1671, when Blood was openly on the government payroll.[17] Although they have misled some writers in the past, these letters must be discounted from any consideration of the spying question during the 1660s.

The case against Blood now rests on two other documents. The first is Joseph Williamson's personal address book, in which he writes of information coming to him from a 'Mr. T. B.', who was in Zeeland in the United Provinces in 1666. The relevant entry states: 'Mr. T. B. fró Holl Zealand writing under ye address of Jo. Taylor at ye Post House London & of Thomas Harris'.[18]

The second document is Blood's own pocketbook, which seems to suggest that he was in the United Provinces around the date given in Williamson's address book. Blood was there with John Lockyer on their trip to persuade Edmund Ludlow to enlist assistance in a rebellious plot. The question is whether we can take it that Joseph Williamson's mysterious 'Mr. T. B.' is in fact Thomas Blood. Was Blood supplying the government with information during the 1660s when he was supposedly a rebel on the run?

The fact that Blood took on the disguise of a doctor has also raised suspicion, as this was a cover often used by spies. Spies would use this particular identity since movements in and out of a doctor's house at any time of the day or night would not appear unusual, and in addition doctors tend to have more access to people's secrets.[19] Of course, a doctor would also be a good cover for a rebel on the run.

Supplying information to the government while being outside the law oneself was not an unknown activity in the Restoration period. Playing the roles of spy and outlaw simultaneously could be profitable. It is true that people in Blood's situation often spied on their peers for their own ends. There could be much to be gained in the form of money, freedom from capture, or even sometimes one's own life. It has been said that a shrewd outlaw, which Blood undoubtedly was, could have given the government stories for years with 'just enough truth to make them plausible, and just enough vagueness to make them unusable'.[20]

We will probably never be able to prove for certain whether Blood was supplying information to Arlington and Williamson in the 1660s. I am not persuaded that he was a spy at this period on the basis of the 'Mr. T. B.' reference. An examination of the events in his life prior to his arrest for stealing the Crown Jewels does not suggest the actions of a spy. Would a spy working for the King twice attempt an attack on the Duke of Ormonde, set a prisoner like Mason free and then steal the Crown?

There is also ample proof in the records that the authorities were actively trying to capture Blood in the years after the Dublin Plot. When Blood was involved in planning an attack in 1665/6, the Earl of Orrery advised Ormonde on how best to capture him and his accomplice: 'As Blood and Aires go under assumed names, it is best to have them watched at the brewers house by some who know their faces well. Otherwise they may escape the search . . .'.[21]

If Blood had been working as a spy since the 1660s it would be surprising for Williamson to have made the enthusiastic comment in 1671 that 'God has made us masters of Blood' when he was finally arrested. He would not have said this about a man who had already been on their payroll for years. Blood's actions during the 1660s were motivated by his religious convictions and not by a need to serve the government.

15

A DUTIFUL SERVANT

The deal had been struck and Blood was now working for the King. Since part of his duty entailed observing the activities of those involved in subterfuge and plotting, he did not move away entirely from his old world. Blood would have been well aware that this was a dangerous environment, inhabited by many unscrupulous individuals, vividly described as 'discharged soldiers, crazed ex-ministers, beggars, footpads, thieves, pimps, vagrants and tricksters . . . who were to dominate the political scene with their lies and malice'.[1]

In contrast to this grimy underworld, with his new-found freedom and status as part of the establishment, Blood also began to play his part in court life, spending a considerable amount of time at the Royal Apartments. One T. Henshaw describes having seen him there in August 1671:

On Thursday last in the courtyard at Whitehall, I saw walking in a new suit and periwig Mr. Blood extraordinary pleasant and jocose; he has been at liberty this fortnight; he is nothing like the idea I had made to myself of him, for he is a tall rough-boned man, with small legs, a pock-frecken face, with little hollow blue eyes.[2]

Blood lost no time in using his elevated position in society to garner favour for his family. In 1673 he put forward Thomas junior as being able to 'manage a company' of soldiers, and his youngest son Edmund as being 'fit for an ensign or a sea officer, having been twice to the East Indies'.[3] His growing influence at Court is also indicated by the granting of the offices of Clerk of the Peace and Clerk of the Crown in County Clare, Ireland, to his son Holcroft in 1676. In 1678 he acquired two army commissions for his sons.[4] He also put in a 'good word' for his uncle in County Clare, writing to Lord Arlington in April 1672: 'I beg your Lordship's remembrance of my uncle Dean Blood's advance in Ireland, that has been Dean 30 years, and was with the King at Oxford, and was an active person.'[5]

In 1673, Blood tried to add to his property when the question of the ownership of the Holcroft estate arose. Maria Blood's brother Charles Holcroft, who had inherited the estate on the death of their father, died and left no heir. Blood was quick to make a claim on the estate by petitioning the King but he was unsuccessful and the estate passed instead to another relative.[6]

One of Blood's principal responsibilities under the agreement made with the authorities must have been the giving of information regarding his old comrades. Many of the hand-written notes of Joseph Williamson include references to information received from Blood during this period. Perhaps it was no coincidence that soon after his pardon three of Cromwell's captains and twenty-four or -five so-called irreconcilables were arrested. He wrote the following to the Duke of York about a man called Smith:

He has been concerned in most conspiracies that have been these 14 years. He was with me in the business of Ormonde, and the business miscarried because he, though appointed, did not follow him, so there needs no proving of this. Then, though he was not one of the fighting party at the taking of the crown, he was employed by me as a scout and has often boasted of it. He was not one of those that went with me to the rescue of Mason, but, I suppose, was one that drudged about getting our horses and tackling ready, and that he has also boasted of. When all my party accepted the King's pardon, he did not, being a Fifth Monarchy person but a wet one. Of late he has been very busy in joining new designs, Colonel Scot, Peyton and Padsell and the rest of that crew being all one, contriving to assassinate persons and to surprise others, and in order to this he was sent by this gang into Westminster about a month since and lay as a spy for ten days counterfeiting his name and had correspondents of that gang . . .[7]

Knowing the amount of information he was in possession of, it is no surprise that many of his old comrades from the militant Nonconformist community were very alarmed by the 'turning' of Blood. Ludlow was one, for example, who was worried about Blood's knowledge of subversive activities. Others, such as Captain William Poveye, who used the alias William Thompson, openly stated that he should be murdered.[8]

Blood was immensely helpful in Charles's plan to deal once and for all with the thorny issue of Nonconformist prayer meetings. The Conventicle Act of 1670 had made life very difficult for Non-conformists by declaring it illegal to hold religious meetings of more than five people, under threat of fine. The fine was 5s the first time a person was caught at one of these conventicles and double that for the second occasion. The minister was fined £20 the first time and £40 for the second, while the owner of the building being used was fined £20. Informants were encouraged in their efforts by receiving a third of these fines.[9]

The Conventicle Act caused a split within Presbyterianism,

with those known as the 'Dons' arguing that it was better to abide by the law and those known as the 'Ducklings' resisting it. One of the major figures within the 'Ducklings' was the preacher James Innes. At one stage Innes asked his fellow Presbyterian, Blood, to request the King to grant 'liberty' to the meetinghouses.[10] When Blood refused, Innes took his request directly to the King but got nowhere. However, Williamson was aware that Blood continued to meet Innes in secret. He wrote: 'Blood sees privately and cunningly Ennys and his friends.'[11] At one point Charles warned the 'Ducklings' that if they did not stop their illegal public meetings they would put his plans for the toleration of private meetings at risk. However, the warning seems to have had no effect.

Apart from his widely accepted desire for religious toleration, one of Charles's major aims in granting Nonconformists the right to hold prayer meetings was to win their support for the coming war with Holland. Although he knew that granting any kind of concession to Nonconformists, and even more so to Roman Catholics, would be a very unpopular political move, in 1672 he issued the Declaration of Indulgence under which he could grant licences which allowed Nonconformist ministers to preach and to conduct their worship freely at authorised locations. It was always intended that Blood would play an important role in this process. He was to act as a conduit for the processing of licence applications. Many of the petitions made by him on behalf of his fellow Nonconformists are documented:

18 April 1672
Request by Mr. Blood on behalf of the Anabaptists at Cranbrooke, Kent, for licences for the houses of Thomas Beaty and Alexander Vines, and for Richard Gun as their Minister; and also on behalf of the Anabaptist meeting in Coleman Street . . .[12]

Before 19 April 1672
Request by Mr. Blood for a licence for Mr. Wells, Presbyterian, at Mr. Weston's house, Sheepstreet, Banbury.[13]

1 May 1672
Request by Thomas Blood for licences for Mr. Kitly, Essex, person and house . . . Mr. Gilson, Burntwood, Essex . . . Henry Lever of Newcastle . . . Thomas Crampton of Toxteth Park . . . a meeting house at Kingsland, Middlesex . . .[14]

As usual with Blood, the process is not without some controversy, as the following letters referring to money show:

14 May 1672
From Thomas Blood to William Mascall, Chirurgeon [Surgeon], at Romford
I enclose the licences you gave me a note for. If you need any other places to be licensed, you can have them. There is no charge for them, only it is agreed that 5s for the personal licences be gotten, and the doorkeepers and under clerks should afterwards be remembered by a token of love.[15]

The next letter, dated 16 May 1672, demonstrates unhappiness on the part of a petitioner and seems to include a thinly veiled threat!

From Thomas Gilson to Mr. Mascall, at the Three Conies, Romford
I have had a conceit that Blood has detained the personal licences for me and Mr. Kitely till you send him word of the money he mentions. Therefore, if you write to him, write smartly that we cannot take it kindly to be so disingenuously dealt with, as if he would stop our

personal licences, though he knows us both, and only send down licences for our houses, which signify nothing without a person, and we should have taken it better if he had sent down the personal licences, and left to our courtesy what we would gratify the clerks and doorkeepers with, rather than to have a sum imposed on us, contrary to the King's express command that nothing should be required, and therefore advise him to send down presently the personal licences for us, lest we make our address some other way.[16]

Charles's Declaration of Indulgence was in effect only for a relatively short time before Parliament forced him to cancel it in March 1673, refusing to vote subsidies for the war until he complied. It is fair to say that Blood had played a major part in the implementation of the Declaration by acting as an approachable intermediary through whom Nonconformists could attain their licences.

Blood also used his influence throughout this period to achieve pardons for rebels from the Nonconformist and ex-Cromwellian community. One person whom Blood probably 'brought in' in this way was John Lockyer, who had assisted him in the Mason escape.[17] In a letter written to Lord Arlington in November 1672 he is seen working for the pardon of one William Low of Dublin, whom he describes as a Major in the old army of the Parliament. He writes: 'I brought the gentleman to the king, according to your direction. The king was satisfied in him, and bade me take care about his pardon, in order to which I request your order for a warrant. Hardly anyone that has been pardoned will turn to a better account, for he is a man of parts and esteem in that party in Ireland . . .'.[18]

On 7 April 1675 he writes to Williamson on behalf of a Captain Humphrey Spurway, formerly of Tiverton: 'I send according to your command the enclosed petition and the name and circumstances of the person for whom a pardon is asked . . . His crimes were the same with the common drove of those his Majesty pardoned at my coming out of the Tower, and no other . . .'.[19]

Another responsibility of Blood's under his agreement with the King was to do what he could to persuade his Nonconformist colleagues at home against a pro-Dutch stance during the war with Holland. When war was imminent a declaration was published that required rebels who were abroad to come home and surrender. At least some of those who came back probably did so with Blood's assistance. Two such people, Desborough and Relsey, came home and were given pardons. It was known that they subsequently met with Blood every day in a room kept for them at White's Coffee-House, behind the Royal Exchange.[20]

He also became very involved in intelligence work during the war, using his contacts to get information from Holland.[21] In April 1672 he wrote the following to Lord Arlington:

A person that came through the Dutch fleet last Wednesday saw 63 ships, men-of-war and fireships together, rendezvoused [sic] at the Weling, but could not distinguish how many there were of each. The Zealand squadron was not come, for last Friday I had an account also from thence with this presumpion, that none of their fleet would stir till after [to]day (?) which was their fast day.[22]

In connection with some pamphlets which were being smuggled in from Holland as a part of a propaganda campaign being waged by William of Orange, Blood gave the following information in 1673:

Let the seamen of the packet-boats be searched for them, for 12 are to be sent that way to our friend. The bulk were to be sent to the Spanish ambassador, whose goods are to be searched by persons of the Custom house. They intended to put them in some small casks in barrels of butter (but that is uncertain) to the Spanish ambassador. Let all things to him be inspected.[23]

In the case of rebels who refused to cooperate and did involve themselves in espionage during the war, Blood was invaluable in deciphering and identifying their letters, which were intercepted from the Netherlands. Williamson was very confident of Blood's ability in this area, and wrote, 'Blood knows the key and the hands.'[24]

Blood also used his wider contacts in the radical community to gather information useful to the regime. Williamson made a note in October 1677 of information which he had received from Blood. Blood, according to Williamson, had met with some Fifth Monarchy men and 'Atheists'. He had informed Williamson that he believed the group to be thinking of an attack upon the Tower of London. Williamson, obviously taking the information very seriously, wrote: 'the Tower to be looked to, the Guards to be well looked to . . .'.[25]

Much later, in March 1683, a tobacconist called John Harrison gave evidence of an intended plot that had been foiled by Blood during these years. He quoted one Ralph Alexander as saying that 'a great number of battle-axes or bills with long staves were provided for the design which Blood discovered to his Majesty after his being taken for stealing the crown, which they lodged at a house in Thames Street, but on that discovery knocked off the heads and threw them into the Thames'.[26]

Blood, it seems, did not always act honourably with his informants within the radical community. One man claimed a number of years after the event that he had informed Blood of a plot to murder the King and Queen, the assassins planning to come by water. However, the man claimed that although Blood had been rewarded for the information himself and, as he heard, had been instructed to reward him, he never received anything![27]

The importance of Blood's work for the regime at this time is underlined by Williamson's letter to the Lord Chancellor of Ireland in January 1678, in which he explains why Blood would not be able to attend to some business before the Chancellor in Ireland. He says: 'the king has commanded me to signify to you that the said Blood is detained here on his particular service and by his command'.[28] The Lord Chancellor's reply to Williamson on the matter reassures him that he 'shall take the best care I can that he suffer nothing therein by his absence on his Majesty's commands'.[29]

A similar letter was written by the King himself to the Lord Lieutenant of Ireland in June 1678, in which he speaks for Blood's son Holcroft: '. . . whereas Holcroft Blood has been absent from Ireland most of the time since he has been in possession of the offices of the Clerk of the Crown and Peace in Clare, he has been so absent by the king's particular licence and command and has remained in England on the king's service'.[30] This came in reply to a petition from Blood to the King in which he explained that there was a law or custom in Ireland under which if the holder of a position such as 'Clerk of the Crown and Peace' left the kingdom without the prior permission of the Chief Governor his position could be forfeited.[31]

One dubious man of the moment with whom Blood can be tenuously linked is Titus Oates, the fanatical Anglican clergyman best known for his creation of the Popish Plot of 1678/9. There is evidence that both Blood and Oates had frequented the club of the Justice of the Peace, Sir William Waller, at Westminster Market Place.[32] Also Blood, it seems, at one stage tried to wreck Oates's credibility by planting some damning documents on him.[33]

In 1678 Oates denounced a plot to the Privy Council which, he fictitiously claimed, was conceived by the Jesuits, who intended to have the King assassinated and

England placed under Catholic rule by means of a Roman Catholic army from the continent. He claimed to have found all this out while posing as a Roman Catholic convert in two Jesuit seminaries. It was true that he had managed to gain admittance to the seminaries at Valladolid and St Omer and was in fact expelled from both. Although the Popish Plot was nothing more than a creation of his imagination, it was successful in engendering fear in the country and resulted in a widespread wave of anti-Catholic sentiment. One of Oates's claims was that a list had been drawn up of all the prominent Protestants who were to be assassinated, a list which included the Duke of Buckingham.

One event which added greatly to the credibility of the Plot and the general feeling of fear among Roman Catholics was the violent death of Sir Edmund Bury Godfrey. Godfrey was a businessman and Justice of the Peace in the London parish of St Martin-in-the-Fields who was known to have had a favourable attitude towards Roman Catholics. In September 1678 Oates had made a sworn deposition of his evidence before him. Godfrey is reported to have made the statement at the time that if there were any truth in the plot 'he himself would be knocked on the head'.[34] He was soon found dead in a ditch on Primrose Hill, stabbed with his own sword and with strangulation marks on his neck. To make matters worse it was claimed that his clothes were covered in candle wax, suggesting the involvement of priests.[35] An opportunist and fraudster called William Bedloe then arrived on the scene claiming that he had been offered £4,000 by the Roman Catholics to dispose of Godfrey's dead body.

As the story spread, the fact that Oates was the only witness to the plot did not prevent his evidence being accepted by the public at large. Neither did it seem to matter that he had a very dubious personal history, having been expelled from the Merchant Taylors' School in London, imprisoned for perjury while a curate and once dismissed as a navy chaplain for misconduct. He was ably assisted in his activities by another rogue called Israel Tonge.

The level of suspicion and paranoia continued to grow until Roman Catholics were being removed from positions of trust, and even the King's brother, the Duke of York, felt the need to resign from the Privy Council and go abroad on account of his Roman Catholicism. During this period many Catholics were arrested and some executed. One outlandish rumour circulating at the time was that a large number of monks had already been shipped in from Jerusalem to sing at the celebrations once the Roman Catholics had seized power.[36]

A small sub-committee, of which Buckingham was a member, was entrusted with the responsibility for investigating the plot. As accusations flew in all directions, even the Queen herself was not spared, Oates claiming that he had heard her give consent for the execution of her own husband!

It seems that Charles himself was dubious about the veracity of Oates's tale from the beginning. He is reported to have laughed when Oates named a man called Bellasis as Commander-in-Chief of the Roman Catholic army as in fact the poor man was bed-ridden. Oates also failed to answer many of Charles's questions convincingly. For example when the King asked him where the Jesuit College in Paris was and Oates replied that it was near the Louvre, Charles said that 'he was as much out as if he had said Gresham College stood in Westminster'.[37]

In the hysterical atmosphere created by the Popish Plot some prominent Roman Catholics decided that the best way to counter its effects was to blame it or a similar plot on the Protestants. James Netterville, a Catholic Irishman who had been a clerk in the Court of Claims in Dublin and also an informer of the Lord Treasurer, Danby, was enlisted to help achieve this.[38] While incarcerated in the Marshalsea for debt in 1679,

Netterville offered another Irishman, Captain Bury, four or five hundred pounds if he would assist in a scheme to blame the Popish Plot on the opposition and in particular to implicate William Bedloe. Unfortunately for Netterville, Bury went straight to Blood with the information. Blood's instructions to the Captain were to continue his association with Netterville in order to find out who was supplying the money. The information that Bury eventually came back with was that the financial backer was a servant to the French ambassador named Russell. When Netterville subsequently confessed his side of the story to a Catholic priest it differed in that he claimed that the intention had actually been to bribe Blood himself with £500.[39]

Another shady character involved in this underworld and with whom Blood was linked was one Thomas Dangerfield. Dangerfield, as a result of various criminal activities including the counterfeit of coins, had been in gaol for a large part of his adult life. It was said that he even once robbed his own father. In 1679 he managed to ingratiate himself with a Catholic midwife named Elizabeth Cellier, who helped him to get out of prison. Cellier was one of those prominent Roman Catholics who, along with Lady Powis, was keen to counter the effects of the Popish Plot. She was known to have once had a relationship of some kind with the murdered Justice of the Peace, Sir Edmund Bury Godfrey.[40]

Once released from gaol, Dangerfield quickly began to involve himself in this world of sham-plot creation. He began to spread rumours of the formation by the opposition of a rebel army, even coming up with documents, most probably forged by himself, in which Shaftesbury and Buckingham were implicated. Blood was also named as a Major-General in this proposed rebel army, as was Sir William Waller. Dangerfield managed to make contact with the Duke of York, who encouraged him in his espionage and even gave him money. Dangerfield got as far as showing his evidence to the King, who passed him on to Secretary of State Coventry.

At this stage he felt it necessary to come up with some additional evidence and so produced some letters that he had stolen from Shaftesbury, which were intended to implicate him further.[41] Dangerfield asked the authorities to raid the house of Colonel Roderick Mansell, who was steward to the Duke of Buckingham. However, he failed in his efforts to persuade Coventry to pursue the matter further.

Undeterred, Dangerfield persisted in spreading tales of the formation of this rebel army. In October 1679 at the Hoop Tavern, Fish Street Hill, he made the acquaintance of one Mr Thomas Curtis, a former MP from Lancashire. Curtis was down on his luck and spent most of his time drunk. During one of their drinking bouts together Dangerfield, having plied him with food and drink, persuaded Curtis that there would be a reward for him if he could get some of the rebel army commissions which were on offer. Curtis's naïve search for the commissions brought him to the Heaven Tavern in Old Palace Yard, Westminster, where he confided in Jane Bradley, the barmaid. He mentioned the name of Thomas Blood, unaware that this tavern was one of Blood's favourite haunts and that Mrs Bradley was a loyal informant of Blood's.

Once she had reported the story to Blood, he instructed her to try to get more information from Curtis. Blood duly reported the matter directly to the King. Charles was in agreement with Blood's strategy of trying to find out more. Eventually Curtis was brought before a justice of the peace and committed to the Gatehouse gaol.

In the meantime Dangerfield had not been idle. He was busily involved in what was to become known as the Meal Tub Plot. He managed to get into the house of Buckingham's steward, Colonel Mansell, under false pretences and there planted some incriminating forged documents behind the bedstead. He then informed customs officials that there were smuggled goods hidden in the Colonel's house. He even accompanied them on their search and when they were about to give up, he miraculously produced the forged papers from their hiding place with the exclamation, 'Here is treason!'[42]

However, his treachery was to no avail when Colonel Mansell brought his case directly to the Privy Council. Under severe pressure, Dangerfield decided to betray Mrs Cellier and turn King's witness. A search of Mrs Cellier's house was undertaken and 'a paper book ty'd with ribbons' was found hidden at the bottom of a tub of meal (hence Meal Tub Plot).[43] The document, which was probably planted by Dangerfield, outlined the whole plot and Mrs Cellier's part in it. In the end his testimony was not believed and the widow was acquitted. In 1685 Dangerfield was pilloried and whipped after being convicted of libel. He died shortly afterwards as a result of a blow he received to the eye from a barrister's cane.

As time passed Blood's credibility with Nonconformists began to falter as they began to see him as part of the establishment rather than as one of their own. Although perhaps inevitable, it had concerned Williamson since the very public pardoning of Blood had first been arranged. In a note dated December 1671 he speaks of Blood being 'lost with the phanaticks'.[44]

16

OLD COMRADES DIVIDED

After so many years spent on the run, Blood was, no doubt, enjoying his new life. However, the details of his former life coupled with the perceived irregularity of his pardon and the nature of his work for the King were sure to earn him enemies both within and without Court. In a time of so many real and sham plots it required the skills of a tightrope walker to sway safely between the many dangerous and treacherous individuals and groups. By the end of the 1670s there were many who would have been happy to see the demise of Thomas Blood. As it happened, it was the souring of Blood's relationship with a dangerous friend that was to prove his undoing.

By this time relations between the Duke of Buckingham and the King had become strained once again. Charles would have been aware of the rumours linking the Duke with Blood's previous criminal activities and perhaps even of his aspirations towards the throne. Not helpful to relations between them was the fact that the one-time maid of honour to Princess Henrietta, Louise de Kéroüalle, now mistress to the King, bore a grudge against the Duke. Some time earlier Buckingham had planned to encourage a romance between her and the King and to that end, after Princess Henrietta's death, he persuaded Louise to accompany him to England. However, having brought her as far as Dieppe he left her there, promising to send a royal yacht to fetch her. When the keenly anticipated yacht never arrived, Louise understandably felt much aggrieved. In her influential position she would be no advocate for the Duke.

Added to all this was the fact that the scandal of his relationship with Lady Shrewsbury continued to give ample ammunition to Buckingham's enemies. An incident had occurred in 1673 in which Lady Shrewsbury's coachman became involved in a fight with a member of the Royal Horse Guards and was killed by the soldier. When the soldier was brought before Buckingham for him to adjudicate on the matter, the Duke showed his partiality by beating him severely.[1]

In addition there was Buckingham's well-known opposition to the Duke of York's marriage to the Catholic Mary of Modena. Feeling isolated, he decided to turn secretly to Louis XIV for help. He requested that Louis send over a representative to discuss with him plans for promoting French interests among some of the MPs. Although Louis agreed to this secret arrangement he told his representative to keep Charles informed of every detail.

By January 1674 the Duke found himself standing before a House of Commons which demanded answers to many accusations, including those regarding the treaty that had been signed with the French. Buckingham was also cross-examined on the promotion of Roman Catholicism in the form of the Declaration of Indulgence and the marriage of the Duke of York to Mary of Modena. Added to all this there was the charge of levying an army without constitutional sanction.[2] Although Buckingham strove to defend himself in his own confident and inimitable style, the process concluded with Parliament requesting that the King 'remove the said Duke of Buckingham from all his employments that are held during His Majesty's pleasure and from the Councils for ever'.[3] The Duke was thus dismissed from the Privy Council.

At this low point in his life a petition regarding his relationship with Lady Shrewsbury was presented to the House of Lords by the trustees and relatives of the late Earl of Shrewsbury's son. They warned of the danger of this relationship for the young heir and ominously spoke of 'conduct even more unnatural than that already ascribed to Lady Shrewsbury'.[4] The Duke was brought before the Lords to answer for his actions, including the duel fought between himself and the late Earl. The petition was supported openly by the Duke of Ormonde.

During the course of this inquisition Buckingham's wife was very upset and was reported by Lord Conway to be 'crying and tearing herself'.[5] She requested leniency not only on her husband's behalf but also that of her rival's.[6] For her part, Lady Shrewsbury, through a letter read by her father, begged that she not be made 'desperate'. Perhaps these requests had some influence on the Lords because they decided that the matter could be resolved by the Duke of Buckingham and Lady Shrewsbury being bound, under penalty of £10,000, to renounce any intercourse with one another. Buckingham publicly acknowledged to the Houses of Parliament 'the lewd and miserable life he had led' and he was seen the following Sunday attending religious service at St Martin-in-the-Fields accompanied by his wife.[7] Thus ended one of the most notorious adulterous love affairs of the century.

Buckingham found himself out of favour and removed from all his previous honours, even the Chancellorship of the University of Cambridge, which he had worked so hard to attain. After about a year spent in the countryside away from the centre of power he returned to become an effective leader of the opposition to the new Test Act introduced by the Danby administration in 1675.

By 1677 he was back in trouble and committed to the Tower as a result of comments he made about the House of Lords in an attempt to have Parliament dissolved. After repeated appeals to the King he was soon free again. During the Popish Plot Buckingham was one of those who supported the exclusion from office of the Duke of York and it was even rumoured that he was prepared to lead a rebellion.[8]

In 1680 news came to light of a plot to do even more serious damage to Buckingham by accusing him of the capital crime of sodomy. Although this accusation was commonly used in the seventeenth century in order to discredit an enemy, rumours of the Duke's guilt in this area had clung to him throughout his career. These rumours were sufficiently rife for him to write denying them.

This particular plot could have originated with the Lord Treasurer, Sir Thomas Osborne, Earl of Danby. Danby had been a leading light at Charles's court and was in fact made Earl of Danby on the strength of being the first Lord Treasurer in Charles's reign to achieve a level of income over expenditure. If he was the instigator of the plot against Buckingham, by the time it came to fruition he was in deep trouble himself.

Danby's trouble began with Ralph Montague, the English ambassador to France. Montague tempted royal disapproval when he had an affair with Barbara Villiers in Paris in 1678, but he made a mistake of much greater proportions when he decided to have a romantic dalliance with Barbara's daughter, Anne. An angry Barbara went straight to Charles to complain and when Montague followed her, leaving his post without permission, he was dismissed from all his positions by an equally angry King. The dispute escalated when Montague decided to get himself elected to the House of Commons and both Charles and Danby tried unsuccessfully to prevent him.

In 1678 the King had asked Montague to consult an astrologer in Paris who had served him well on a previous occasion. Barbara now claimed that Montague had told her that he had corrupted the man into giving the predictions that suited his own ends. This revelation resulted in Montague's arrest on a very dubious charge of treason.[9] However, Montague struck back by producing some incriminating documents at the House of Commons, which referred to Danby's involvement in secret negotiations conducted with Louis XIV.

Danby now found himself in trouble and having to answer six articles of impeachment. Since Buckingham had come to hate Danby just as much as he had Clarendon and Ormonde in earlier years, he was very keen to be involved with his impeachment. Apparently Danby became aware of this and threatened Buckingham 'with a counter charge of a personal nature' if he did so.[10] Danby also remarked to Lord Ossory that he was 'not out of hopes of procuring something very material against the Duke'.[11] These threats may have been effective, as the Duke did not take a leading role in the impeachment debates that followed.

When Danby was eventually removed from power and incarcerated in the Tower, a plot against Buckingham materialised in which a charge of a very 'personal nature' was made against him. In the absence of the Lord Treasurer himself the plot could have been carried forward by his steward, a disgruntled ex-employee of Buckingham's, Edward Christian. Christian had been Buckingham's rent-collector and later chamberlain but the Duke had dismissed him for embezzlement of estate funds. He could have provided the money needed for this plot against his old employer.

It is uncertain whether Danby was involved in this plot against Buckingham, but one man who found himself right in the middle of it was Buckingham's old comrade, Thomas Blood. Perhaps something had happened to cause a rift between these two villainous characters who had lately been allies.

On 20 January 1680 Blood was called before the anti-court magistrate Sir William Waller, an old enemy of his, and asked to answer for his involvement in a plot against the Duke of Buckingham. Two scruffy Irishmen called Philemon Coddan and Samuel Ryther were present and they stated that they had been engaged to give evidence that Buckingham had sodomised a girl called Sarah Harwood and subsequently forced her to go to France. They had a statement, which they said had been prepared for them to sign, giving details of the Duke's crimes. In addition, the case against Buckingham was to be strengthened by a young man named Philip le Mar who was to swear that he had also been sodomised by the Duke. Le Mar's mother, Frances Loveland, was also to act as a witness. Coddan and Ryther were naming none other than Thomas Blood as the chief instigator of this plot against the Duke's good name. Their version of events was supported by a man named Jenks who was an employee of Buckingham's. Also present was Buckingham's solicitor, Mr Whitaker, another of Blood's enemies.

According to the evidence of these men various meetings took place in the back rooms of a number of disreputable inns at which attempts were made to persuade them to swear against Buckingham. Another Irishman called Maurice Hickey also became involved. Hickey's main function was to help persuade Coddan and Ryther to cooperate. This proved quite difficult with Ryther in particular, who was not cooperating. Thomas Curtis then appeared on the scene, apparently having switched sides and out on bail. As Hickey was experiencing some difficulties with Ryther, Curtis was now called on to help. Coddan and Ryther claimed that Curtis was working for Blood.[12] Curtis tried to persuade Ryther to cooperate, and large amounts of money were offered to both men. Blood was said to have been in attendance at one of these meetings himself and to have questioned Ryther on what exactly he would swear to. Ryther's reply on that occasion was that he would swear to anything they wanted him to.[13]

Eventually it seemed that Ryther was persuaded and everything was set to go ahead. At the next arranged meeting in Bloomsbury, Hickey brought the prepared statement for both men to sign, in which Buckingham's crimes were graphically detailed. The statement read:

Whereas Samuel Ryther and Philemon Coddan Gentlemen, in St. Martins Parish in the Fields, do hereby confess and declare, That Sarah Harwood of the City of London, Gentlewoman, did confess before us, That the Lord Duke of Buckingham was with his Privy Members as far in both her Privy Parts as he could go with forcible entrance, stopping her Breath, and that the said Lord Duke of Buckingham hath since conveyed the said Sarah Harwood out of the way, by which means the King lost his Evidence. And do further declare, That since that time, the said Duke did order the said Sarah to be murdered, and since the time is murdered or sold beyond Sea. And do further declare, that the said Duke hath committed the said Sin of Sodomy, with several more, which we are ready to prove, when we are required as the Kings Evidence.

However, only Ryther turned up at this meeting and when he was shown the statement he absconded with it. Coddan and Ryther then went straight to Buckingham's solicitor, Mr Whitaker, with the document and were duly brought before Sir William Waller. We do not know if the Irishmen had changed sides or had been playing a double game from the beginning. Apart from any money being offered to them, they did have other motivation to attack their former employer Buckingham, who owed them money.[14]

Having heard Coddan and Ryther's story Waller expressed himself satisfied with it and advised Blood that he should find two people willing to put up bail for him. The following morning Blood returned to Waller's house, refused to put up bail and demanded to see a copy of the *mittimus* so that he could know what he was charged with. When Waller advised him against this course of action Blood told him 'that he would insist upon being treated by him according to the form of Law'.[15]

The following day, Saturday, a constable was sent to Blood's house but Blood was in bed and sent his man to inform Waller that he would come later.[16] Blood attended to some business he had at court that day but on his way home he met a constable at the upper end of King Street in Westminster who informed him that he had a warrant against him. In fact what the constable actually had in his possession was a *mittimus*. He asked Blood if he wished to go somewhere so that they could discuss the matter out of the public gaze. They went to the Dog tavern where he showed Blood the relevant document.

It read:

To the Keeper of the Gate-house Westminster, or his Deputy.

Whereas Oath hath been made by two Witnesses before me, That Collonel Thomas Blood is a Confederate in the late Conspiracy of suborning Witnesses falsly to accuse and charge his Grace the Duke of Buckingham of Sodomy, he having refused to give in Bail to appear the next General session of the Peace to be held for the City and Liberty of Westminster to answer the Premisses.

These are therefore in His Majesties Name upon sight hereof to direct you to take into your Custody the Body of him the said Collonel Thomas Blood, and him safely to keep until he shall be delivered by due course of law.[17]

Later that day, when Waller sent his man to find out what had happened, he was surprised to find that the constable was with Blood at the Dog tavern. Waller had assumed that Blood had been brought straight to the Gatehouse gaol. However, the somewhat irate constable informed Waller's man that he had told Waller earlier that he could not bring Blood to gaol until he was issued with a warrant from a Justice of the Peace. Furthermore, since he was effectively holding Blood prisoner without the proper authority, he was very worried. In fact two of his acquaintances, who were also constables, had informed him that 'it is in the Power of Mr Blood to bring me under great trouble, for my inadvertency in the thing'.[18] He also made it clear that, without a warrant, if Blood expressed a desire to leave he would not hold him 'one minute longer'.[19]

Although this discussion between the constable and Waller's man took place in a separate room, Blood, shrewd as ever, figured out what was going on. When the constable returned, Blood told him that he was aware that he was being held unlawfully and that although he knew the constable was 'a neighbour, and a civil man' he might have to bring 'an action at law' against him, and make him pay so much an hour for false imprisonment.[20]

At that moment the necessary warrant arrived:

To all constables, and other His Majesties Officers Civil and Military.

Whereas Oath hath been made by two Witnesses, That Collonel Thomas Blood has been a Confederate in a late Conspiracy of falsly accusing and charging his Grace the Duke of Buckingham, of Sodomy, and has refused to give in Bail for his appearance at the next General sessions to be held for the City and Liberty of Westminster.

These are therefore to will and require, That you Seize and apprehend the said Collonel Thomas Blood, and if he shall refuse to give in Bail, to carry him, and deliver him into the Hand of Mr Church, Keeper of the Gatehouse in Westminster, according to the Tenor of the Mittimus in your hands.[21]

At six o'clock that evening, which was the earliest a Justice of the Peace could be found, Blood gave in bail. His version of events differed greatly from that being put forward by his accusers.[22] He was adamant that he had not been involved in any plot to tarnish the reputation of the Duke of Buckingham. According to him the whole exercise was designed purely to hurry him to gaol, to expose him to public scandal and to strip him of the good esteem of his friends. In his version of events, on or about 21 January 1680 Mrs Jane Bradley of the Heaven tavern informed his servant, John, that she had some information to impart to his master. Blood came to see her and Mrs Bradley told him that she was very worried that a plot was in train against the government. When Blood enquired why she thought so, she replied that a few nights previously she had 'two shabby fellows here . . . that told me, they had something of great consequence, in reference to the welfare of the publick, to reveal, but that they did not know how to do it . . .'.[23]

Mrs Bradley asked Blood to return at six o'clock that evening because, although she had not told them his name, she had arranged for him to meet these two men. When Blood arrived, Mrs Bradley told him that the men were present and that from 'their behaviour, whisperings and ill aspects' she judged them to be rogues.[24] She also told him that when Curtis, who had been drinking with them, told them that it was Mr Blood that they were to meet, one of them said, 'Is that the Blood that stole the Crown? God damn him, we will have nothing to do with him, for he is a great Friend of the Duke of Buckingham's.'[25]

They then announced that they had to leave, but Mrs Bradley managed to persuade one of them to show himself to Blood as it would look bad for her if it appeared that she had lied about the appointment. One of them then went to Blood and told him that they had indeed a matter of importance to discuss but that they could not discuss it on that particular evening. They would, however, meet with him the following Monday morning and tell him 'what we are privy to'.[26] The man then left with a group of others who Blood judged to be 'very shye' to appear to him. This, according to Blood, was his first ever meeting with these men.

He had been at home for about an hour that night when Mrs Bradley arrived. She once again repeated her reservations about the men, saying that she believed them to have 'some mischievous designs upon him' and advised him that he should protect himself against them. From Blood's evidence their conversation went as follows:

Blood: 'What will you have me do to strangers that I never saw before?'
Mrs Bradley: 'Do seize, carry, and get them examined before one of his Majesty's Justices of the Peace, where they must upon a report of this meeting, and what they told me touching a Plot, give a satisfactory account of what they are, and what they mean, or are privy to, relating to a Plot.'[27]

According to Blood, he decided to act on Mrs Bradley's advice and went in search of a Justice of the Peace. He first went to a Colonel Walcup, who was out of town. Next he met with Dr Chamberlain, to whom he told his story. He requested a warrant to have these two men, Coddan and Ryther, seized and examined to determine what their intentions were. Dr Chamberlain acceded to his request.

Blood and Dr Chamberlain, accompanied by 'a constable or two, and a competent number of watchmen',[28] set off to find the two men. Having spoken to them both at their respective lodgings, they seized them at eleven o'clock at night at Ryther's place in Soho. Dr Chamberlain questioned them on their knowledge of a plot, on their reason for seeking a person to whom they could confide and their refusal to discuss the matter with Mr Blood that evening at the Heaven tavern. Whereas Ryther insisted that he knew nothing of the matter whatsoever, Coddan did say that they had wished to discuss the Duke of Buckingham, who owed them wages, and that they needed someone who could 'cope with him'.[29] Dr Chamberlain said that he believed this to be nothing more than an excuse.

At one point in the examination, according to Blood, one of them stated that he would have revenge on the Duke of Buckingham and that he would swear sodomy against him. Thomas Curtis was present at the time and he stated that he had heard the men talk of a plot against the government. On the question of that evening in the Heaven tavern they said that they had refused to speak to Blood on account of his friendship with the Duke.

Dr Chamberlain had a second encounter with them the following Monday morning at his house. On this occasion they were accompanied by Mr Whittaker and Mr Jenks. This time they admitted that they did know something of a 'Design . . . relating to the welfare and Good of the Publick, but would come to no particulars'.[30] Obviously making no progress, Dr Chamberlain dismissed them.

Blood stated that on 20 January Sir William Waller's servant came to his house and asked him to come to the Buffalo-Head tavern near the Gatehouse in Westminster. Blood thought that he was being invited to drink a glass of wine. However, when he got there he found waiting for him Waller, Coddan, Ryther, Mr Whittaker and Mr Jenks. Blood was shocked at how well dressed Coddan and Ryther were on this occasion when compared to the state in which they had appeared before Dr Chamberlain just a short time before: 'fine Rigging, such as neat Clothes, good Perriwigs, new Hats, clean Linnen, Swords and all other Accoutrements answerable, so that Mr Blood did scarce know them . . .'.[31]

According to Blood's account, after a few glasses of wine Waller got to the point of the meeting: 'I am troubled at the misfortune you have lately brought yourself under,' he began, ' not only because you are a neighbour and a long acquaintance but for other reasons, which I shall not mention.' 'What misfortune do you mean?' replied Blood much surprised. 'I do not understand you!' 'These two gentlemen are come hither before me, to depose upon oath, that you as a confederate have attempted at several times to corrupt them by money, and the prospect of other considerable rewards, to swear and falsely to accuse and charge his Grace the Duke of Buckingham with sodomy.' 'How!' replied Blood. 'What is the matter? I don't know what you say.' 'Mr Blood,' interjected Coddan at that point, 'you would suborn us to swear buggery against the Duke of Buckingham.' 'O shame on you,' said Blood, 'can you be so impudent as to invent such a thing of me, that is a stranger to you, and who never saw you in his life, but before Dr Chamberlain and one time at Heaven?'[32]

It was at this point that Coddan and Ryther were backed up in their accusation by Whittaker and Jenks. This was the first time that Blood had heard anything of the matter of accusing the Duke of Buckingham of sodomy. He expressed himself to be much shocked by the accusation, and declared those others present who were willing to swear to the honesty of Coddan and Ryther to be enemies of his. He stated that the paper in which the Duke was accused of the crime was an invention of their own.[33]

On 30 January Waller had Mrs Bradley brought before him.[34] According to Blood's account, Waller did not like the two people she brought to stand bail for her and therefore sent her straight to gaol. However, the constable brought her instead to the house of a Mr Church until she could arrange for bail to the value of £200 the following day.

Now that Mrs Bradley was in trouble, an acquaintance of hers came forward about a fortnight later and swore that she too had heard these men, Coddan and Ryther, speaking together that night in the Heaven tavern when they had come to meet Blood. She swore on oath that she had heard them say, 'We will do this Rogue Blood's business for him, and get Oaths enough to swear against him by that time Sir William Waller comes to Town.'[35] She told her story to a friend the following day and this friend swore to it before the Justice as well.

With what he felt to be growing evidence in his favour, Blood desired that his two accusers be bound over to answer charges that he wished to bring against them. However, Waller refused to cooperate in any way with Blood or to bring them forward. By this time his relations with Blood had been damaged even further by some disparaging comments Blood had made about him around town. Blood's information was that Coddan and Ryther could not be found and so he decided to act on the matter himself, declaring:

Whereas Philemon Codan and Samuel Ryther pretended Servants to his Grace the Duke of Buckingham, did falsly asperse Thomas Blood Esq; that he would have suborned them to swear some notorious Crimes against the said Duke, (who now absconded themselves.) If any can give notice of the said Philemon Coddan and Samuel Ryther, unto the said Thomas Blood Esq; at his House over the Bowling-Alley in Westminster, or to Dorman Newman at the Kings-Arms in the Poultry, they shall be well rewarded.[36]

This was not long 'cried' around the streets before a Mrs Stringer, who sold ale at the end of Long Acre, came forward with information. She knew Coddan because he owed her money for drink. She said that he had lived for some time in the house of a 'dyer' called Mr Monk and was now at a 'Shoomakers in Walbrook'.[37] Blood had both Mrs Stringer and the dyer brought before a Justice of the Peace to testify on oath.

Mrs Stringer testified before the Justice that she knew all three, Coddan, Ryther and Hickey. They were, she asserted, 'all three constant Companions together' and had spent a considerable amount of time drinking in her cellar. They often met there with other Irishmen and, when they did not want their conversation to be overheard, spoke among themselves in the Irish language.

She also said that the day after word went out about Blood's reward for the capture of Coddan or Ryther, she saw Hickey running past her window. Since he owed her money she ran after him. When she caught up with him she noticed that he was sweating, with every drop of perspiration 'as big as a pea'.[38] He told her that he was going to see Mr Coddan, and he assured her that they would both be in a position to settle their bills very soon. She gave evidence that she saw Coddan herself a number of times after that but failed to get any money out of him.

Mr Monk for his part gave evidence that he thought Coddan, Ryther, Hickey and the rest of their gang were rogues. He also said that Coddan often told him that he and Blood had never conversed together in their lives.[39] Monk later told Waller the same when called upon to do so.

Eventually an indictment was drawn up against Blood and a number of others in which it was stated:

The Jury for our Lord the King present upon their Oaths; That Maurice Hickey . . . otherwise called Maurice Higgens . . . Robert Smith . . . otherwise called Robert Jones . . . John Haley . . . Thomas Curtis . . . Thomas Blood, late of the Parish of St. Margaret Westminster, in the County of Middlesex, Gent. Edward Christian . . . Arthur Obrian . . . Philip le Marr . . . And Jane Bradley . . . The seventeenth day of March . . . at the Parish of St. Martins in the Fields, in the County of Middlesex aforesaid, unlawfully, unjustly, nequitiously, devilishly and corruptly, by unlawful ways and means between themselves, have practised, conspired, intended and designed, to dispoil and deprive his Grace the Duke of Buckingham, then and there one of the Peers and

Grandees of this Kingdom of England, not only of his honour, estimation and reputation, but also to take his life away, and destroy his life and dignity of Dukeship. And to cause the said George Duke of Buckingham, to be taken, arrested and condemned to death, for detestable Crimes and Offences of Sodomy and Buggery, by him supposed to be committed, with one Sarah Harwood, and divers other persons, against the order of nature. And also for inticing or transporting of the said Sarah Harwood beyond Sea, to suppress and take off their Evidences, of and concerning the Crimes of Sodomy and Buggery aforesaid.[40]

The indictment goes on to state that the accused persons did 'perswade, procure' and 'suborn' Coddan and Ryther by using 'Wine, Junkets and other alurements'. They also used 'great sums of money' and offered 'divers great advantages and preferments'. They had 'given, deposited, and paid down to' Coddan and Ryther 'divers sums of money'. To Coddan they had paid 'forty pounds of lawful money of England' while Ryther received fifty. Furthermore Coddan was promised 'the friendship and respects of some Peers and men of Power and Degree, And also should have a Place or Office in and about the business of the Customs of our Lord the King, now called a Land-waiter's place, of the yearly value of two hundred pounds, and the sum of sixty pounds in money's numbred, and a certain maintenance during his life'.

Similarly Ryther was also promised the same friendship of 'some peers' and of men 'of great Estates and Degree'. He was also offered 'a Place or Office in or about the Custome House Business of our Lord the King . . . also money to redeem his Estate Mortgaged by him . . . being above three hundred pounds. And three hundred pounds more . . .'. Ryther, according to the indictment, was offered an additional £300 in the form of a purse of gold to get him to sign the statement against the Duke.

Although such a valuable bribe was offered, according to their story, Coddan and Ryther decided to forgo this and do the honourable thing by telling the truth instead.

Blood saw that the venues being named for the alleged meetings were the Crown in Ram Alley in Fleet Street, and the Bear in Holborn. He claimed never to have been in either place. According to him, in order to back up his claim he brought 'five substantial people' to both places to enquire about him. These people were told by those present that they did not know Blood, they had never seen him, and that as far as they knew he had never been at either premises. Furthermore, he claimed that it was nonsense to accuse him of working together on a plot with Mr Christian since it was well known that they did not even like each other: 'It is very improbable that he should coact with one in an Intreague of this make, to whom he always grudged the civility of drinking either publickly or privately.'[41] He further claimed that if any house in England of good repute could give evidence that he had been seen in the company of Mr Christian he would 'acquiesce under the severest censure'.[42]

At this remove it is hard to determine who was telling the truth in this convoluted story. There are a number of options. It is possible that Coddan and Ryther were telling the truth and Blood did play a major role in this plot to ruin the Duke of Buckingham. In this case the whole scheme would probably have been sponsored by someone else. That person could have been Danby or Christian, as already suggested, but it could equally have been any of the other people who harboured a resentment against Buckingham. Perhaps at the last moment Coddan and Ryther decided to recant out of fear when pressurised by the magistrate, or maybe they double-crossed Blood because they had been 'bought' by a higher bidder. Then again, Blood could have been completely innocent of these charges and framed by Coddan and Ryther. If this was the case the person at the back of it could have been anyone from a disgruntled Non-conformist to someone annoyed at Blood's pardon and presence around Court. In any event, Sir William Waller was an all too willing participant in the conviction of Blood, perhaps blinded to any pursuit of justice by his personal hatred of Blood. Blood's own version of events is composed to make him look innocent and to emphasise his friendship with the Duke of Buckingham.

Understandably, this scandalous case caused a sensation, with one observer remarking that 'the business of the Duke of Buckingham is now become the only discourse of the town'.[43] At the trial, which took place before a jury at the King's Bench bar, Blood continued to protest his innocence vehemently. Claims and counter-claims of perjury and bribery were thrown in all directions. However, notwithstanding his version of what had happened, the jury found Blood guilty of blasphemy, confederacy and subornation. Also found guilty were Christian, Curtis and Hickey. All were severely fined and imprisoned.

Philip le Mar and his mother were also tried and found guilty. Le Mar was unable to attend his trial through illness.[44] It seems that a botched attempt was made by someone to get him to change his story by drugging him. One document refers to the incident: 'it's discoursed that who have any ways been tampering with Le Marr or abetting to it, will be made public exemplaries for such their ill practices'.[45] He died soon afterwards and his unfortunate mother was forced to stand in the pillory for her part in the plot. It is documented that she was 'severely dealt with by the people throwing dirt and rotten eggs at her'.[46] Mrs Bradley of the Heaven tavern was found to be innocent of any involvement in the affair.[47]

Although Sir William Waller had been successful in achieving this very gratifying victory over Blood, ultimately the affair ruined his career. His enthusiasm for the conviction had led him to indulge in tampering with witnesses and bribery, even spending a whole night drinking with Hickey when the Irishman was supposed to be in gaol. This gave the King a welcome excuse to remove his commission as a Justice[48] and he later fled to the Netherlands.[49] Coddan appears as a tide-surveyor in Plymouth in 1685.[50] It is possible that this position was given to him as a reward for his evidence against Blood.

As if the guilty verdict was not bad enough for Blood, his situation grew even worse when Buckingham, looking for revenge against his old comrade, brought a defamation charge known as a *Scandalum Magnatum* against him and was awarded £10,000 in damages.

We can only wonder how the Duke of Ormonde reacted when he first received the news of this dire change in circumstances for his old enemy. He may have first heard of the verdict in a letter written to him by a Francis Gwyn in which he is told: 'the Grand Jury found the bill against one Mr Christian, O'Brien, Blood and some others for a contrivance of endeavouring to suborn witnesses against the Duke of Buckingham'.[51]

17

TO MEET DEATH UNAFRAID

Blood's life now lay in ruins. He remained in gaol for months, unable to find the money necessary to secure his release. On this occasion there was no influential patron such as the Duke of Buckingham eager to engineer his release, nor was he in a strong bargaining position as he had been in 1671. Although he had experienced many difficult times in his life before, the situation in which he now found himself was worse, coming as it did just as he had managed to achieve some level of comfort for himself and his family.

He had no option left now but to plead with a number of influential people for assistance. One of these people was the Duke of York. Blood sent one of his sons to request assistance from James on his behalf and followed up that visit with a letter in which he wrote:

The great favour you expressed towards me, when my son was with you yesterday, requires the greatest return of acknowledgement I am capable of . . . I requested that on this fob action, in case I could not find bail, his Majesty would encourage some to be bail for me . . . I therefore humbly beg that I may not be left in this cause to fall . . .[1]

He claims in the same letter that he had been targeted for this action because he kept 'the Commonwealth party in awe' and because he brought about the downfall of Sir William Waller.

He wrote in a similar vein to Secretary Jenkins in the same month in which he claimed that the Duke of Buckingham and all the Commonwealth party want 'to get me out of their way, knowing that I have been a check on their disloyal actions these 9 years and remain so still'.[2] He also told the Secretary that he was 'quite destitute' and 'would entreat you to encourage some persons to be bail for me'.[3]

Finally the requested money arrived from an unknown source and Blood was released on bail in July 1680. He claimed that the charge of *Scandalum Magnatum* being brought against him by Buckingham was illegal and that he was determined to fight it.

Unfortunately, by this time the 62-year-old Blood seems to have been considerably weakened by the whole experience. He returned home from gaol to his house at the Bowling Alley, Westminster,[4] as a man in a most difficult situation. It must have been hard for him, having come through many vicissitudes in his life and having finally managed to elevate himself and his family to a comfortable place in society, to be now facing financial ruin. This time he could not solve his problems by daring action. As one seventeenth-century writer put it, Blood, 'by the circumstances he was in then, found no probability of getting out of the mire by his former methods of contriving and daring, but perceived himself in a manner manacled at this time, whereas in all the other exigencies of his life he had constantly trusted to his hands and action'.[5]

Thus we are told that Blood fell into an uncharacteristic 'pensive passion of Melancholly'.[6] This was brought on, no doubt, by the situation in which he now found himself. He fell rapidly into an illness that progressed until it became clear that the end of his life was approaching rapidly. One minister of religion who visited him stated that 'he found him apparently in a sedate temper of mind as to the concerns of his Soul, nothing startled at the apprehensions of approaching death; that he told him he had set his thought in order, and was ready and willing to obey when it pleased God to give him the last call'.[7]

Such was his lethargic condition at the end that some who saw him even suggested that he had taken some form of narcotic to hasten his death.[8] This view may have been no more than a reaction to the shock felt by those who had always known him as an energetic and spirited man of action. 'On Monday before his death he was taken speechless, and continued so, in a kind of Lethargie, without much motion or action unless a drowsie heaving and fetching for breath.'[9]

Thomas Blood died on Wednesday 24 August 1680 at around 3 p.m., about two weeks after first falling ill.[10] He had stated before the end that he met death 'unafraid'.[11] His body was laid to rest on the following Friday in the graveyard of New Chapel, Tothill Fields.

After his death a rumour was started, which would have outraged Blood and been incredible to all those who knew him, to the effect that he had died a Papist.[12] If we know anything of the man this at least is one rumour we can readily dismiss.

However, his death was not quite the end of the story. As with many heroes and villains who are larger than life, once he was dead, the story began to circulate that his death had been nothing more than a ruse and that he was in fact still alive. Blood, it was believed, was up to one of his old tricks. He was planning to slip away and escape the rigour of the law once again. The authorities decided that there was only one way to quell this rumour, and orders were given for the body to be exhumed and identified.

A coroner and jury were appointed to examine and identify the body. On the Thursday following his funeral his body was disinterred from its resting place. Although the jury was composed mostly of people who had known Blood in life, his face was reported to have changed so much, and was so swollen, that they had great difficulty agreeing to his identity. Even when a captain who was present showed them the enlarged thumb that Blood was known to have they were not totally convinced.[13] Finally, however, they did agree on the identity of the body and Blood was once again laid to rest.

The adventures of Colonel Thomas Blood were finally at an end, although his reputation was to live on:

> Here lies the Man, who boldly hath run through,
> More Villanies than ever ENGLAND knew;
> And nere to any Friend, he had was true,
> Here let him then by all unpittied lye,
> And Let's Rejoyce his time was come to Dye.[14]

18

A LIFE OF EXTREMES

By now the body of Thomas Blood had been buried, exhumed and reburied, and people were gradually beginning to accept that this infamous figure was really dead. They began to realise that this time it was no clever trick. He was not in hiding, waiting to commit some outrageous crime of which the newsletters would give full and entertaining accounts.

Blood had lived a life of extremes. From enjoying property and wealth as a Protestant under Charles I in Ireland, he found himself drawn into bloody wars in Ireland and England, during which he fought both for and against the King. Another period of relative comfort during the Cromwellian era was followed after the Restoration by his involvement in revolutionary plots, acts of rebellion and life as an outlaw on the run. When his execution seemed almost inevitable he managed to turn the tables and find himself in comfort once again at the Court of Charles II. But even then, as his life was nearing its end, the good times were not destined to last. Instead of living out his days quietly he became, either as victim or instigator, the focal point of the notorious case involving the Duke of Buckingham's reputation, which led to his ultimate downfall and death.

Despite his demise, the memory of Blood's deeds has

lived on, although popular representations of his life have tended to become rather one-dimensional. The incident for which he is best known, the theft of the Crown Jewels, has led to him being remembered simply as some kind of daring highwayman. But if Blood is to be fully understood he must be placed within the religious context of the seventeenth century. A fanatical loyalty to Protestant Non-conformity informed his life. He was involved in what he saw as a just fight against a concerted effort to stamp out his religious identity. With the collapse of the Commonwealth and the restoration of the monarchy Blood and the other Nonconformist 'phanaticks' like him found themselves ousted from power and position. Throughout his reign Charles II and his government had to take the activities of these people very seriously. They tried to control the situation in a number of ways: arresting those identified as potentially dangerous, using informers wherever possible, attempting to locate illegal religious meetings and searching for the sources of seditious literature.

Although he is known for stealing the Crown Jewels, Blood was a rebel and not a thief. He was not motivated by financial gain, but was working 'for ye Lord's cause'.[1] His main aim was to get religious freedom for Nonconformists, which he achieved at least temporarily when involved in acquiring licences for his co-religionists under the short-lived Declaration of Indulgence of 1672.

Religious fervour alone does not cause someone to lead an extreme life like Blood's. There were many devout Protestant Nonconformists who took no part in any form of militant activity. Blood was a man with an almost pathological desire for excitement and infamy combined with extreme religious fervour. His yearning for risk and danger is perhaps best exemplified by the theft of the Crown Jewels. Even to become as involved as he did with the notorious Buckingham suggests a kindred spirit. He probably found that element of danger attaching to the

Duke alluring, although it ultimately turned out to be disastrous for him.

For Blood the life he led was justified and made bearable by a strong belief in his religious cause. But how was it for his loved ones? We can only imagine how difficult it was for his wife, Maria, coming as she did from as dignified a background as Holcroft Hall. She was drawn by her husband into a world for which she was ill prepared. When she left Holcroft Hall for Ireland with her husband and young baby she must have hoped for a life of comfort. Instead, for much of her married life she was forced into uncertainty, frequently on the move, and with no property or wealth. To rear her children in this way, with a father who spent much of their childhood on the run, cannot have been easy. It must have been hard for her when her husband, having managed to escape what seemed like certain execution and having been restored once again to property and standing in society, was ruined as a result of the Buckingham affair. After Blood's death Maria seems to have lived out the rest of her life in quiet anonymity.

There is one humorous account on record that recalls a probably fictitious meeting between Maria Blood and an infamous highwayman called Thomas Wilmot. The story goes that one day as she was travelling on the Lincoln stagecoach it was held up by Wilmot. Maria pleaded with the highwayman to treat her kindly on the grounds that she was only a defenceless woman. However, Wilmot was unimpressed and replied, 'Madam, the falsehood of women has been the only cause of my misfortunes . . . You are all false, perfidious and perjured . . . As you are a woman, madam, you must expect no favour from my hands, who am a professed enemy to the whole species. Therefore, dear Mrs Blood, be pleased to deliver your money this moment, or I'm afraid blood will come of it the next.'

The story tells how when she offered him half-a-crown Wilmot snapped angrily: 'You saucy bitch, do you think I will be put off with half-a-crown, when nothing less than a whole one would satisfy your husband when he robbed the King?' On searching her he found around fifteen guineas and a silver thimble.[2] Since Wilmot was hanged in 1670, it is impossible that he could have made reference to the stealing of the Crown in this way.

The effects of Blood's life on his eldest child are clear. Thomas junior was involved in many of his father's dubious enterprises, including the attempt on Ormonde in London when he was only around nineteen, and the theft of the Crown Jewels shortly afterwards. He developed his own career in more 'common' crime and operated as a highwayman under the name of Thomas Hunt. Some might see this involvement in highway robbery as a natural extension of the activities carried out with his father, but this is not how Blood senior saw it. It was Blood's firm belief that his own activities were 'for ye lord's cause', but he was critical of his son's illegal activities, or 'wickedness' as he called it.[3] Thomas junior married a woman named Frances Delafaye and they had one son. He is said to have emigrated to America, but it seems he may have died before his father since he is not mentioned in Blood's will.[4]

Of the other Blood children, we know that William became a steward on HMS *Jersey* in 1679 and died at sea around the year 1688. Edmund also went to sea on HMS *Jersey*, where he was a purser. He died in 1679. Unfortunately we know little of their brother Charles except that he went to the Duke of York in 1680 to speak on his father's behalf, who was languishing in gaol at the time in connection with the Buckingham affair. Charles continued to correspond with James after his father's death.[5] The girls, Mary and Elizabeth, both married, becoming Mrs Corbett and Mrs Everard respectively.

There was at least one son on whom his father's career does not seem to have had any adverse effects. In 1679, with the help of his father, Holcroft Blood was appointed a 'Clerk of the Crown and Peace' for County Clare in Ireland.

From there, obviously inheriting his father's love of excitement if not his roguish ways, Holcroft joined the military and was promoted through the ranks until he became the Principal Artillery Commander of the allied forces in the War of the Spanish Succession.[6] He died on 19 August 1707 and although he had no children by his wife Elizabeth, he did father an illegitimate child, also called Holcroft, by a Dutch woman named Dorothy Cooke.

What of those other figures who had played such important roles in the life of Thomas Blood? The Duke of Ormonde was appointed Lord Lieutenant of Ireland for the third time in 1677, and raised to a Duke in the English peerage in 1682. In spite of these honours his final years were not easy. A tragic blow struck him in 1680 when his loyal son, the Earl of Ossory, was seized by a high fever and, despite treating him by bleeding him profusely and placing pigeons at his feet, the doctors failed to save him.[7] In the mid-1680s Ormonde's beloved wife also died. On the King's death Ormonde was removed from the Lord Lieutenancy of Ireland. By the late 1680s he was suffering repeated bouts of painful gout and was finding it impossible to attend Court in his capacity as Lord Steward. He died at Kingston Lacy in Dorset in 1688 and was interred in Westminster Abbey.

The already poor reputation of the Duke of Buckingham, despite a favourable verdict in the highly publicised court case, had been tarnished beyond redemption. He spent the last years of his life away from the seat of power at his estate in Yorkshire, paying only occasional visits to Court. On 16 April 1687 he died in the bed of one of his tenant farmers in Kirkby Moorside, where he often stayed while out hunting. As the end neared he wrote: 'To what a situation am I now reduced! Is this odious little hut a suitable lodging for a prince? . . . I am forsaken by all my acquaintances, neglected by the friends of my bosom.'[8]

By the mid-1680s the Merry Monarch was also nearing the end of his life. One morning in 1685

Charles II fell seriously ill. The bleedings and other efforts of his physicians only seemed to add to his pain and discomfort. On his deathbed he gave consent to his brother James to fetch a priest and while most people were asked to leave the bedchamber he finally fulfilled his promise to convert to Roman Catholicism.[9] Four days after the illness had first struck, he died.

On Charles's death his brother duly became James II. Those who opposed the succession of a Roman Catholic took solace from the fact that by early 1688 James was fifty, with a childless second marriage. They reassured themselves that the Crown would return to Protestant hands on his death, with the accession of James's daughter by his first marriage, Mary, and her Dutch husband, William of Orange. However, later that year their worst fears were realised when James's wife gave birth to a son and heir.

Shocked by this development, seven prominent individuals took the bold step of inviting Mary and William to take the throne immediately. This took place by means of the Glorious Revolution of 1688 without any effective opposition from James. He did mount a fight in Ireland with the support of the French and Irish Catholics, most notably at the Battle of the Boyne in 1690, but he was defeated and a new era had begun.

APPENDIX

AN ELEGIE ON CORONEL BLOOD,
Notorious for Stealing the Crown, &c.
Who Died the Twenty Sixth of August, 1680.

Thanks ye kind Fates, for your last Favour shown
Of stealing BLOOD, who lately stole the Crown;
We'l not exclaim so much against you since;
As well as BEDLOE, you have fetcht him hence,
He who ha been a Plague to all Mankind:
And never was to any one a Friend,
Nay to himself such torment was at last,
He wisht his Life had long ago been past.
For who can bear a discontented minde
Or any Peace with an ill Conscience finde,
Thro' his whole Life, he practis'd Villany
And Lov'd it though he nothing got thereby;
At first uneasy at the Kings return
With secret malice his bold heart 'did burn.
Against his Sovereign, and on pretence
He had much wrong'd his Feign'd Innocence;
To IRELAND went, and several ways did try
Rather then he would unrevenged Dye,
To vent his Malice on His MAJESTY.
But finding there all his attempts prove vain,
To ENGLAND forthwith he returns again,
And after some small time, he had Liv'd here
The first Great thing in which he did appear,

Was rescuing from Justice CAPTAIN MASON,
Whom all the WORLD doth know, t'have been a base one
The next ill thing he Boldly undertook,
Was Barbarously seizing of a DUKE.
Whom as he since confes'd, he did intend
To Hang for Injuries he did pretend:
The DUKE had alone him, though the World does know
His Grace was ne're to a Good Man a Foe:
Having through all, his many well spent Days;
Serv'd His KING and Country, several ways
And Patiently his troubles underwent,
Finding a sweetness, ev'n in Banishment
And Death, he Patiently wou'd have endur'd,
The KINGS Restoring cou'd he have secur'd:
A DUKE, who being by Providence preserv'd
Hath begot Sons; who Valiantly have serv'd.
His MAJESTY, and Great Renown Obtein'd.
In many Battles by your valour Gain'd,
Great OSSERY, who by his Conduct wise,
Did Oft by Stratagems, his Foes surprize
And hath as often beat them with his Sword;
Was the Eldest Son, of this most Noble LORD.
But I my HEROE almost had forgot,
And th' next thing he Engag'd in was a PLOT.
To seize the CROWN; and without doubt he who
So Great a Piece of Villany would-do,
When he saw Time, wou'd have attempted too;
HIS MAJESTY; but failing of the prize,
About the Town he undiscover'd lies,
Harbour'd by some of's fellow Rogues, yet see
How few can scape concernd in Villany,
In a short time, he apprehended was
And brav'd His MAJESTY, even to his Face
Yet when one wou'd, have thought he should have had;
Reward for's Villany; and have been made
Example to all Ages our good King,
Gave him his Life, (who long has strove to bring

Destruction on him,) and did him Restore
To liberty, thinking he ne're wou'd more
Do any thing unjust again when loe;
His stiring Spirit, was not contented so,
For he Engages inth' Conspiracy,
To ruine th' Honour, Life, and Liberty,
Of a deserving Noble Honest Peer,
And had Him brought, unto destruction near
But Divine providence for ever Blest:
Prevented this, as well as all the Rest
By th' coming in of some, that were concern'd
Which all your PLOT; into confusion turn'd,
At last our Famous HEROE Coronel BLOOD,
Seeing his Projects all will do no good,
And that Success was to him still deny'd,
Fell sick with Grief, broke his great Heart and dy'd.

THE EPITAPH.
Here Lies the Man, who boldly hath run through,
More Villanies then ever ENGLAND knew;
And nere to any Friend, he had was true,
Here let him then by all unpittied lye,
And Let's Rejoyce his time was come to Dye.
FINIS.

London, Printed by J.S. in the year, 1680.

NOTES

All references are given in full in the bibliography. Abbreviations used in notes are as follows:

BL: British Library
CSP: Calendar of State Papers
HMC: Historical Manuscripts Commission
PRO: Public Record Office

Prologue

1. *London Gazette*, Monday 8 May to Thursday 11 May 1671. Spelling and capitalisation have been amended for ease of reading.
2. Ibid.

Chapter One

1. Abbott, p. 6.
2. Burke; Montgomery-Massingberd; Blood, p. 2; Weir, pp. 26, 27; MacKenzie, J., unpublished paper on the Blood family consulted at Local Studies Library, Ennis, County Clare.
3. Blood, pp. 2, 3; MacKenzie, J., unpublished paper on Blood family at Local Studies Library, Ennis, County Clare.
4. CSP, 1671–2, pp. 372, 373.
5. There is a stone tablet in Kilfernora Cathedral, County Clare, that names the younger Neptune, describing him as a grandson of Edmond Blood from Derbyshire who settled in Ireland in 1595 and was MP for Ennis in 1613.
6. Blood, p. 3.
7. See Kaye.
8. For details of the Blood family genealogy see Burke and Montgomery-Massingberd.

9. *Remarks*, p. 1.
10. I am using the term Anglicanism although it did not come into general use until after 1660. See Davies, *The Isles, A History*, p. 559.
11. Ibid., p. 574.
12. Reilly, p. 16.
13. Davies, *The Isles*, p. 579.
14. Morrill, p. 27.
15. Reilly, p. 30.
16. Coote, p. 57.
17. *The Civil Survey AD 1654–1656*, vol. V.
18. Both were committed Protestants, according to Kaye.
19. BL Add. MS 36916, fo. 233; Marshall, *Intelligence and Espionage*, p. 187.
20. Ibid., p.187.
21. Petherick, p. 14.
22. CSP, Ireland, 1666–9, p. 88.
23. Frost, p. 369.
24. Reilly, p. 22.
25. He would later change sides once again following the execution of Charles I and fight with the Royalists and Roman Catholics, so many of whom he had killed just a short time before.
26. Kaye, pp. 10, 11.
27. Burghclere, *Ormonde*, vol. I, pp. 322, 323.
28. Kaye.
29. Burghclere, *Ormonde*, vol. I, p. 431.
30. Ibid., p. 429.

Chapter Two

1. This chapter draws mainly on Kaye and Rylands.
2. Kaye, p. 15.
3. Newchurch parish register, as cited in Kaye.
4. Ibid.

Chapter Three

1. Kaye, pp. 162, 163.
2. For more on Titus Oates and the Popish Plot see Chapter 15.
3. Bodleian Library, Rawlinson MS A185, fos 473, 474.
4. Ibid.

5. Ibid.
6. Ibid.
7. Marshall, *Intelligence and Espionage*, p. 204; PRO, SP 19/294, fo. 139.
8. Bodleian Library, Rawlinson MS A185, fos 473, 474.
9. Abbott, p. 94.
10. Burghclere, *Ormonde*, vol. II, p. 14.
11. Arnold, p. 37.
12. Carte, vol. IV, pp. 74–5.
13. Burghclere, *Ormonde*, vol. II, p. 17.
14. Arnold, p. 87.
15. Hutton, p. 196; Burghclere, *Ormonde*, vol. II, p. 59, from *History of Ireland* by Father D'Alton, vol. II, p. 371.
16. Burghclere, *Ormonde*, vol. II, p. 64 quoting from CSP, Ireland, vol. II, p. 23, speech of Sir A. Mervyn.
17. Hutton, p. 149.

Chapter Four

1. This copy was later sent by the Lord Lieutenant to the Irish House of Commons; *Life and Adventures*, p. 6; Greaves, *Deliver Us*, p. 144.
2. Burghclere, *Ormonde*, vol. II, p. 67.
3. Bagwell, p. 36, from 'A Narrative by Sir Theophilus Jones, etc.', Trinity College MSS f. 3, 18 (no. 47) 01.
4. Greaves, *God's Other Children*, p. 21.
5. *The Horrid Conspiracie*, p. 5; Greaves, *Deliver Us*, chapter 5, note 34.
6. *Report on the Manuscripts of the Marquis of Ormonde*, p. 251; Bagwell, p. 37; HMC, Report VIII, pp. 623, 624 (Trinity College MSS).
7. *Report on the Manuscripts of the Marquis of Ormonde*, vol. 2, pp. 252, 253.
8. Herlihy, p. 45.
9. Bagwell, p. 37.
10. Greaves, *Deliver Us*, p. 144.
11. *The Horrid Conspiracie*, pp. 7–9.
12. Ibid., pp. 13–15.
13. Ibid., pp. 10, 11.
14. Ibid., p. 11; CSP, Ireland, 1663–5, p. 99.
15. *The Horrid Conspiracie*, p. 12.

16. CSP, Ireland, 1663–5, pp. 111, 112.
17. Sir James Barry's speech at the trial of Captain Blood.
18. CSP, Ireland, 1663–5, pp. 176, 177; Bagwell, p. 38; Greaves, *Deliver Us*, pp. 148, 149.
19. Ibid., p. 149.
20. *The Journal of the House of Commons of the Kingdom of Ireland*, vol. II, p. 330.
21. Ibid.
22. Ibid., p. 340.
23. Ibid., p. 354.
24. Ibid., pp. 347, 350.
25. *Remarks*, p. 2.
26. For details of the Lecky escape see Burghclere, *Ormonde*, vol. II, p. 73; CSP, vol. II, p. 294.
27. Greaves, *Deliver Us*, p. 149; Marshall, *Intelligence and Espionage*, p. 140.
28. *Report on the Manuscripts of the Marquis of Ormonde*, vol. 2, p. 252.
29. Ibid., vol. 4, p. 251, Letter from Ormonde to Earl of Anglesey.
30. Ibid., vol. 5, p. 81, Letter from Ormonde to Earl of Longford.
31. CSP, Ireland, 1663–5, p. 100.
32. Burghclere, *Ormonde*, vol. II, p. 106.
33. Greaves, *God's Other Children*, p. 86.
34. Hutton, p. 207.
35. Greaves, *God's Other Children*, p. 87.
36. *Report on the Manuscripts of the Marquis of Ormonde*, vol. 4, p. 251, Letter from Ormonde to Earl of Anglesey.

Chapter Five

1. CSP, 1663–4, p. 405.
2. HMC, Report VIII, p. 523.
3. See Marshall, *Intelligence and Espionage*, pp. 198–200.
4. Carte, pp. 138, 139.
5. CSP, 1664–5, pp. 259, 260.
6. Ibid., p. 259.
7. Greaves, *Enemies*, p. 11; PRO, SP 29/102/36, 97.
8. Greaves, *Enemies*, p. 11.
9. *Remarks*, p. 4.
10. Ibid., p. 5.
11. *Life and Adventures*, p. 8; *Remarks*, p. 5.

12. Bodleian Library, Rawlinson MS A185, fo. 474.
13. CSP, Ireland, 1663–5, p. 662; CSP, Ireland, 1666–9, pp 25, 26, 33, 34.
14. Greaves, *Enemies*, p. 39.
15. Ibid., p. 106.
16. CSP, Ireland, 1666–9, pp. 25, 26, 33, 34.
17. Greaves, *Enemies*, pp. 39, 40.
18. Ibid., p. 106.
19. CSP, Ireland, 1666–9, p. 33.
20. CSP, 1665–6, p. 243.
21. Greaves, *Enemies*, p. 41.
22. *A modest Vindication of Oliver Cromwell from the Unjust Accusations of Lieut-Gen. Ludlow* (1698), p. 2, as quoted in Marshall, *Intelligence and Espionage*, p. 189.
23. *Remarks*, pp. 3, 4.
24. Ibid., p. 4.
25. Ibid., p. 3.
26. CSP, 1666–7, p. 64.
27. See Greaves, *God's Other Children*, p. 92.
28. CSP, Ireland, 1666–9, p. 214.
29. According to Marshall, *Intelligence and Espionage*, p. 209, Israel Tonge was the person who spread this rumour.
30. Greaves, *Enemies*, p. 5.
31. Ibid., p. 75, although his name does not appear on the proclamations listing the main rebels.
32. Bodleian Library, Rawlinson MS A185, fos 473, 474.
33. CSP, Ireland, 1666–9, p. 88.
34. CSP, 1667, pp. 1, 2.
35. Greaves, *Enemies*, p. 75.

Chapter Six

1. Mason's correct title was 'Colonel Mason' but he was usually known as 'Captain Mason'.
2. Greaves, *Enemies*, p. 193.
3. CSP, 1667, p. 326.
4. Ibid., p. 337.
5. For Darcy's opinion see CSP, 1667, p. 337 and for Blood's see *Remarks*, p. 8.
6. CSP, 1667, p. 337.
7. Ibid., p. 337.

8. See Chapter Fourteen.

9. CSP, 1667, pp. 326, 337.

10. For this claim of poisoning made by Leving's friend, William Freer, see Marshall, *Intelligence and Espionage*, p. 167.

11. Ibid., pp. 156–68 for an account of Leving's activities.

12. *Remarks*, p. 8.

13. Ibid.

14. This account of the Captain Mason escape is based mainly upon Blood's version of events. The accounts of Darcy and Leving differ slightly.

15. *By the King. A Proclamation for the Discovery . . .*; see also CSP, 1667, p. 369.

16. Ibid.

17. Picard, L., *Restoration London*, p. 82.

18. HMC, Report VIII and Appendix, p. 158.

19. Ibid.

20. CSP, 1667, p. 326, Leving to Arlington.

Chapter Seven

1. Although the spelling 'Ormond' was generally used prior to the Dukedom of 1661, in the interests of simplicity I have used the spelling 'Ormonde' throughout this book.

2. Burghclere, *Ormonde*, vol. I, p. 13.

3. Ibid., pp. 15, 16.

4. Ibid., p. 29.

5. Ibid., pp. 29, 30.

6. Ibid., p. 28.

7. Carte; Burghclere, *Ormonde*, vol. I, p. 33.

8. Ibid., p. 37.

9. Ibid., p. 36.

10. Ibid., pp. 39, 40.

11. Carte, vol. IV, p. 692.

12. Carte, vol. I, p. 130; Burghclere, *Ormonde*, vol. I, p. 84.

13. Carte, vol. IV, p. 692; Burghclere, *Ormonde*, vol. I, p. 299.

14. Ibid., p. 345.

15. Reilly, p. 19; Burghclere, *Ormonde*, vol. I, p. 81, quoting from J.T. Gilbert, 'Contemporary History of Affairs in Ireland', *The Aphorismical Discovery*, vol. II, part I, p. 55.

16. For the £500 see Burghclere, *Ormonde*, vol. I, p. 407.

17. Bryant, p. 59.

18. Carte, vol. III, p. 627.
19. Burghclere, *Ormonde*, vol. I, pp. 446, 447.
20. Ibid., p. 430.
21. Carte, vol. III, p. 627.
22. Burghclere, *Ormonde*, vol. I, pp. 434, 435.
23. Ibid., p. 438.
24. Carte, vol. III, p. 632.
25. Hutton, p. 111.
26. Carte, vol. IV, p. 1.
27. Ibid., p. 40.
28. Burghclere, *Ormonde*, vol. I, pp. 44, 45.
29. Arnold, p. 87.
30. Ibid., p. 120.
31. Carte, vol. IV, p. 153.
32. Ibid.
33. Ibid., p. 270; Burghclere, *Buckingham*, pp. 158–60; Burghclere, *Ormonde*, vol. II, pp. 125, 126.
34. Carte, vol. IV, p. 311.
35. Burghclere, *Ormonde*, vol. II, p. 141.
36. Ibid., p. 146.
37. Ibid., p. 155.
38. Carte, vol. IV, p. 352.
39. Ibid., p. 352.
40. Bagwell, vol. III, p. 89.

Chapter Eight

1. Bryant, p. 215.
2. HMC, Report VIII, part 1, pp. 154–9.
3. From *Diary*, 1 September 1660 as quoted in G.H. Garter and W.H. Godfrey (eds), *London County Council Survey of London*. London: Country Life Ltd.
4. HMC, Report VIII and Appendix, p. 157.
5. Ibid.
6. Ibid., p. 155.
7. Abbott, p. 15.
8. *By the King: A proclamation. Charles R. whereas upon Tuesday, the sixth of this instant December . . .*
9. *London Gazette*, 5–8 December 1670.
10. Burghclere, *Ormonde*, vol. II, p. 189.
11. HMC, Report VIII and Appendix, p. 154.

12. CSP, 1670, p. 594.
13. CSP, 1671, p. 37.
14. HMC, Report VIII and Appendix, p. 155.
15. CSP, 1665–6, p. 377; CSP, 1666–7, p. 463.
16. HMC, Report VIII and Appendix, p. 155.
17. Ibid.
18. *By the King: A proclamation. Charles R. whereas upon Tuesday, the sixth of this instant December . . .*
19. HMC, Report VIII and Appendix, p. 155.
20. Ibid., p. 158.
21. CSP, 1671, pp. 210–11, 483.
22. HMC, Report VIII and Appendix, p. 157.
23. Ibid.
24. Ibid., p. 155.
25. Ibid., p. 158.
26. Ibid., p. 159.
27. Ibid., p. 155.
28. Ibid., p. 158.
29. Ibid., p. 156.
30. Ibid., p. 157.
31. For the three Hursts see ibid., pp. 155, 156.
32. Ibid., pp. 156, 157.
33. Ibid., p. 157.
34. Ibid.
35. Ibid., p. 159.
36. Ibid.
37. Ibid., p. 156.
38. Ibid.
39. Ibid., p. 159.
40. Greaves, *Enemies*, p. 208.

Chapter Nine

1. Buckingham wrote a number of comedies, e.g. *The Rehearsal* (1671).
2. Bagwell, p. 87.
3. Marshall, p. 216.
4. Burghclere, *Ormonde*, vol. II, p. 187.
5. Morrill, p. 29.
6. Burghclere, *Buckingham*, p. 8.
7. Ibid., p. 10.

8. Ibid., p. 12.
9. Ibid., p. 15.
10. Ibid.
11. Ibid., p. 24; note Ludlow, *Memoirs*, vol. I, p. 255.
12. Burghclere, *Buckingham*, p. 26.
13. Ibid., p. 27.
14. Ibid., p. 28.
15. Bryant, p. 47, tells us that it was Burnet who first made this accusation; however, he disagrees with it, citing lack of evidence. See also Coote, pp. 53, 54.
16. Burghclere, *Buckingham*, pp. 28–30.
17. Ibid., p. 33; Newnham MSS, Earl of Denbigh, Basil, Earl of Denbigh, to his mother.
18. Burghclere, *Buckingham*, p. 55; Sir J. Reresby's *Memoirs*, p. 73.
19. Burghclere, *Buckingham*, p. 59; Clarendon MSS no. 672, Hyde to Nicholas, 2 March 1652.
20. Burghclere, *Buckingham*, p. 65.
21. Ibid., pp. 65, 66; Clarendon MSS, vol. II, 1199.
22. Burghclere, *Buckingham*, pp. 72–3.
23. Ibid., p. 79.
24. Ibid., p. 85 quoting Brian Fairfax.
25. Burghclere, *Buckingham*, p. 88; HMC, 15th Report, part II, p. 48, 25 August 1657, M. Eliot Hodgekin.
26. Burghclere, *Buckingham*, pp. 88, 89; Brit. Mus. Add. MSS 27, 872.
27. Burghclere, *Buckingham*, p. 91.
28. Ibid., p. 96; Fairfax Papers, vol. IV, p. 253.
29. Burghclere, *Buckingham*, p. 97.
30. Dryden, J., *Absalom and Achitophel: A Poem*.
31. Burghclere, *Buckingham*, pp. 102, 103.
32. Ibid., p. 102.
33. Ibid., p. 113.
34. Ibid., p. 119.
35. Ibid., p. 121.
36. Ibid., p. 122.
37. Ibid., p. 134.
38. Ibid., p. 147; John Evelyn's *Diary*, vol. II, p. 322, 19 September 1676.
39. Burghclere, *Buckingham*, pp. 160, 161.
40. Ibid., p. 167, note: *Life of Clarendon*, vol. III, p. 203.
41. Burghclere, *Buckingham*, p. 168.
42. Burghclere, *Ormonde*, vol. II, p. 135.

43. Carte, vol. IV, p. 293.
44. Ibid., p. 293.
45. Ibid., pp. 293–5; Burghclere, *Ormonde*, vol. II, p. 135; Burghclere, *Buckingham*, p. 170.
46. Ibid., p. 174.
47. Ibid.
48. Ibid., p. 175.
49. Carte, vol. IV, p. 295.
50. Burghclere, *Buckingham*, p. 177; BL, Carte MS 48, fo. 488, Ormonde to Clarendon, Dublin, March 1666.
51. Burghclere, *Buckingham*, p. 181.
52. Burghclere, *Ormonde*, vol. II, p. 135.
53. Bryant, p. 192; Hutton, pp. 254, 258, 259, 280 argues that in fact Buckingham was never very powerful and that the real power lay with Arlington.
54. So writes Burghclere, *Buckingham*, p. 188; Hutton, however, fundamentally disagrees with this: see previous note.
55. For example Fraser, pp. 255, 256: 'Nor did Buckingham assume that total leadership which Clarendon had once enjoyed.'
56. Burghclere, *Buckingham*, p. 194; Samuel Pepys, *Diary*, vol. VIII, p. 11.
57. Burghclere, *Buckingham*, p. 195; St Evrémond to Waller, Letter IV, quoted in Thomas Longueville, *Rochester, and other Literary Rakes of the Court of King Charles II*, London: Longman and Co., 1902, p. 94.
58. Burghclere, *Buckingham*, pp. 196, 197; CSP, 1667–68, pp. 192, 193, quoted by Pepys.
59. Burghclere, *Buckingham*, p. 198; Samuel Pepys, *Diary*, vol. VIII, p. 18.
60. Burghclere, *Buckingham*, p. 180.
61. Ibid., pp. 206–9.
62. Ibid., p. 211.
63. Bryant, p. 211.
64. Fraser, p. 275.
65. Ibid. says that they signed it. This treaty remained a secret to most people until revealed by Lingard in 1830.
66. Hutton, p. 280.
67. Burghclere, *Buckingham*, pp. 209, 210.
68. Ibid., p. 244.
69. Bagwell, p. 87.
70. Petherick, p. 33; Burghclere, *Buckingham*, p. 242.

Chapter Ten

1. Younghusband, p. 14.
2. Ibid., p. 16.
3. According to Younghusband, p. 101; Fraser puts the amount at over £30,000 with reference to Plumb, *Royal Heritage*; see also Hilliam, pp. 137–9.
4. Younghusband, pp. 146, 147.
5. Ibid., p. 47.
6. Ibid., p. 232.
7. Ibid., pp. 128, 129.

Chapter Eleven

1. *Dunboyne, A Picture of the Past*, published by the Old Dunboyne Society, 1993.
2. Petherick, p. 26.
3. *The Dictionary of National Biography*, vol. II, 'Earliest Times to 1900', p. 694.
4. Although I have opted for this spelling of Perrott's name, various versions can be found in the documents, e.g. Parrett, Parret, Parrot, Parrott, Perrot.
5. Marshall, *Intelligence and Espionage*, p. 193, note 41.
6. According to Gilbert Talbot's account in Younghusband.
7. The daggers used by Blood and Perrott in the robbery of the Crown Jewels were believed at one time to be held in the Royal Literary Fund Society's Museum, Adelphi Terrace, according to Abbott, p. 97. A dagger believed to be that used by Blood is now held by the Royal Armouries at the Tower of London.
8. *Remarks*, p. 10.
9. Younghusband, p. 184.
10. For the story of Beckman see Marshall, *Intelligence and Espionage*, p. 175.
11. Younghusband, p. 150.
12. Petherick, p. 29.
13. Abbott, p. 77.
14. Bodleian Library, Rawlinson MS A185, fos 473, 474.
15. Burghclere, *Buckingham*, pp. 314, 367.
16. HMC, Report VIII and Appendix, p. 159.
17. *Remarks*, p. 9.
18. CSP, 1671, p. 351.
19. Ibid.

Notes

Chapter Twelve

1. Bryant, p. 4.
2. Coote, p. 12.
3. Ibid.
4. Ibid., p. 18.
5. Bryant, p. 43.
6. Hutton, chapter 3.
7. Ibid., p. 77.
8. Ibid., p. 87.
9. Ibid., p. 122.
10. Ibid., p. 124.
11. Ibid.
12. Ibid., pp. 185, 186.
13. Ibid., p. 232.
14. Coote, p. 246.
15. Bryant, p. 47.
16. Hutton, p. 97.
17. Ibid., pp. 125, 126.
18. Ibid., p. 77.
19. Ibid., p. 125.
20. Ibid., pp. 186, 187.
21. Bryant, pp. 149, 150.
22. Ibid., p. 158.
23. Ibid., p. 152.
24. Hutton, p. 231.
25. Bryant, p. 169.
26. For an example of such poetry see Bryant, p. 169, 170.
27. Hutton, pp. 262, 279.
28. Bryant, pp. 237, 239.
29. Hutton, pp. 335, 336.
30. Ibid., p. 336.
31. Bryant, p. 248.
32. Hutton, p. 336.
33. Ibid.
34. Bryant, p. 209.
35. Hutton, p. 417.
36. Bryant, p. 164; Hutton, pp. 449, 453.
37. Ibid., p. 453.
38. Ibid., p. 450.
39. Ibid., p. 448.
40. Fraser, p. 194.

41. Ibid.
42. Ibid., p. 193.
43. See Sobel.
44. Burghclere, *Buckingham*, pp. 361, 362.
45. Coote, Preface, p. xi.
46. Hutton, p. 134.
47. Fraser, p. 186.
48. Ibid., p. 189.

Chapter Thirteen

1. *Life and Adventures*, p. 20.
2. Marvell, *Complete Poetry*, p. 193.
3. CSP, Jan.–Nov. 1671, p. 244.
4. Younghusband, p. 105.
5. Petherick, p. 29 for apprentice barber and sinder-woman.
6. CSP, Jan.–Nov. 1671, p. 237, *Newsletter* dated 13 May 1671.
7. Burghclere, *Ormonde*, vol. II, p. 190.
8. CSP, Jan.–Nov. 1671, p. 385.
9. Ibid., p. 409.
10. CSP, Oct. 1672–Feb. 1673, pp. 295, 296, 409.
11. Younghusband, p. 176.
12. BL, Carte MS 69, fo. 164, Blood to Ormonde.
13. CSP, Jan.–Nov. 1671, p. 255; Greaves, *Enemies*, pp. 212, 213;
    the document is PRO, SP 29/290, fo. 11.
14. Marshall, *Intelligence and Espionage*, p. 195, note 50.
15. Abbott, p. 79.
16. Ibid., p. 76.
17. Bryant, p. 218.
18. See Chapter Fourteen.
19. Bodleian Library, MS Eng. Letters d. 37, fo. 84, as quoted in
    Marshall, *Intelligence and Espionage*, p. 186.
20. Greaves, *Enemies*, p. 215.
21. CSP, Dec. 1671–17 May 1672, pp. 8–10.
22. Abbott, p. 84.
23. CSP, Jan.–Nov. 1671, p. 496.
24. CSP, Dec. 1671–17 May 1672, pp. 40, 41.
25. CSP, 1 March 1676–28 Feb. 1677, p. 97.

Notes

Chapter Fourteen

1. See Marshall, *Intelligence and Espionage*, for an excellent work on intelligence and espionage in this period.
2. Burghclere, *Buckingham*, p. 189.
3. Marshall, *Intelligence and Espionage*, p. 50 for Frances; Hutton, pp. 279, 280 for Louise.
4. Marshall, *Intelligence and Espionage*, p. 37. Marshall credits the information on the dismissal to *Lorenzo Magalotti at the Court of Charles II: His Relazione d'Inghilterre of 1668–9*, edited and translated by W. E. Knowles Middleton, Ontario, 1980. Although it is uncorroborated, Marshall does not think that this makes it unlikely.
5. Hutton, p. 321.
6. See Marshall, chapter 2.
7. CSP, 1666–7, p. 64.
8. PRO, SP 9/32, fos. 211–30.
9. Marshall, *Intelligence and Espionage*, p. 128.
10. See Chapter Six; Marshall, *Intelligence and Espionage*, p. 156.
11. PRO, SP 29/102, fos 48–9.
12. CSP, 1664–5, pp. 259, 260.
13. CSP, 1666–7, p. 545.
14. CSP, 1667, p. 427.
15. Marshall, *Intelligence and Espionage*, chapter 3.
16. For more on the Popish Plot see Chapter Fifteen.
17. Marshall, *Intelligence and Espionage*, p. 201. These letters refer to Jonathan Jennings, whose release Blood petitioned for in 1671. It was Lyon-Turner, *Original Records*, III, pp. 218–45, who first suggested this misdating.
18. PRO, SP 9/32, fo. 213; Marshall, *Intelligence and Espionage*, p. 88.
19. Ibid., p. 130.
20. Abbott, p. 56.
21. CSP, Ireland, 1666–9, pp. 33, 34.

Chapter Fifteen

1. Marshall, *Intelligence and Espionage*, p. 207.
2. HMC, Report VIII, Part One, Report and Appendix, p. 370.
3. CSP, Oct. 1672–Feb. 1673, p. 502.
4. Marshall, *Intelligence and Espionage*, p. 207.

5. CSP, 1671–2, pp. 372, 373.
6. Kaye, pp. 250–3; Rylands, pp. 19, 20.
7. CSP, 1 Mar. 1678–31 Dec. 1679, p. 290.
8. CSP, Jan–Nov. 1671, p. 413; Greaves, *Enemies*, p. 214.
9. Ibid., p. 154.
10. CSP, Jan–Nov. 1671, p. 560.
11. Ibid., p. 560.
12. CSP, 1671–2, p. 343.
13. Ibid., p. 348.
14. Ibid., p. 434.
15. Ibid., p. 568.
16. Ibid., p. 589.
17. Greaves, *Enemies*, p. 221.
18. CSP, Oct. 1672–Feb. 1673, p. 111.
19. CSP, 1 March 1672–29 Feb. 1676, p. 56.
20. *Life and Adventures*, p. 22; *Remarks*, p. 11.
21. Abbott, pp. 86, 87.
22. CSP, Dec. 1671–17 May 1672, pp. 372, 373.
23. CSP, Oct. 1672–Feb. 1673, p. 595.
24. CSP, Jan.–Nov. 1671, p. 496; Greaves, *Enemies*, p. 217.
25. CSP, 1 March 1677–28 Feb. 1678, p. 388.
26. CSP, 1 Jan.–30 June 1683, p. 103.
27. Ibid., p. 66.
28. CSP, 1 March 1677–28 Feb. 1678, p. 571.
29. Ibid., p. 601.
30. CSP, 1 March 1678–31 Dec. 1678, with Addenda 1674 to 1679, p. 241, from S. P. Ireland.
31. Ibid., pp. 38, 39; see also p. 237.
32. Marshall, *Intelligence and Espionage*, p. 208; for Blood's attendance at club see *Just Narrative*, p. 6.
33. Marshall, *Intelligence and Espionage*, pp. 208, 209; for the case of these planted letters see the pamphlet by 'T.S.', *The Horrid sin of Man-Catching: The Second Part Or Further Discoveries and Arguments to Prove that there is no Protestant Plot* (1681), p. 20.
34. Burghclere, *Buckingham*, p. 346.
35. Ibid., p. 347.
36. Bryant, p. 272.
37. Ibid., pp. 270, 272.
38. Marshall, *Intelligence and Espionage*, p. 211.
39. Ibid., pp. 211, 212.
40. Ibid., p. 241.
41. Ibid., p. 213, note: Coventry Papers 11, fos 441–2.

42. Burghclere, *Buckingham*, p. 374.
43. Ibid., p. 375.
44. CSP, Dec. 1671–17 May 1672, p. 28.

Chapter Sixteen

1. Burghclere, *Buckingham*, p. 278.
2. Ibid., p. 281; Burghclere, *Ormonde*, vol. II, p. 248.
3. Burghclere, *Buckingham*, p. 288.
4. Ibid., p. 291.
5. Ibid., p. 295, note: *Essex Papers*, vol. I, p. 160, Lord Conway to Earl of Essex, 10 January 1673/4.
6. Burghclere, *Buckingham*, p. 295.
7. Ibid., p. 296, note: Essex Papers, Lord Angier to Lord Essex, vol. I, pp. 167, 174.
8. Burghclere, *Buckingham*, p. 352.
9. Hutton, pp. 364, 365.
10. Burghclere, *Buckingham*, p. 363.
11. Marshall, *Intelligence and Espionage*, p. 217; *Report on the Manuscripts of the Marquis of Ormonde*, vol. 4, pp. 328–9.
12. Marshall, *Intelligence and Espionage*, p. 219.
13. BL Add. MS 28047, fos 67–71.
14. *Remarks*, p. 12.
15. *The Narrative of Colonel Thomas Blood*, p. 8.
16. Ibid., p. 9.
17. Ibid.
18. Ibid., p. 10.
19. Ibid.
20. Ibid., p. 11.
21. Ibid., p. 12.
22. See *The Narrative of Colonel Thomas Blood* for his version.
23. Ibid., p. 1.
24. Ibid., p. 2.
25. Ibid., p. 3.
26. Ibid., p. 4.
27. Adapted from ibid.
28. *The Narrative of Colonel Thomas Blood*, p. 5.
29. Ibid., p. 6.
30. Ibid., p. 7.
31. Ibid.
32. Adapted from ibid., p. 8.

33. Ibid., p. 21.
34. Ibid., p. 14.
35. Ibid.
36. Ibid., pp. 17, 18.
37. Ibid.
38. Ibid., p. 19.
39. Ibid., p. 20.
40. Ibid., pp. 24–8.
41. Ibid., p. 28.
42. Ibid.
43. CSP, 1 Jan. 1679–31 Aug. 1680, p. 431.
44. Ibid., p. 489.
45. Ibid., p. 432.
46. Ibid., p. 521.
47. Marshall, *Intelligence and Espionage*, p. 222, note 171.
48. Ibid., p. 221.
49. Ibid., p. 223.
50. Marshall, 'Colonel Thomas Blood and the Restoration Political Scene', *The Historical Journal*, 32, 3 (1989), p. 573 gives the following references: CSP, 1682, pp. 47–8; CSP, 1690–1, p. 458; Calendar of Treasury Books, 1685, pt. I, pp. 116, 149.
51. *Report on the Manuscripts of the Marquis of Ormonde*, vol. IV, p. 275, letter from Francis Gwyn to Ormonde, 14 February 1679/80.

Chapter Seventeen

1. CSP, 1 Jan. 1679–31 Aug. 1680, p. 556.
2. Ibid., p. 560.
3. Ibid.
4. *Remarks*, Postscript, p. 1.
5. Ibid.
6. Ibid.
7. Ibid., p. 2.
8. Ibid.
9. Ibid.
10. Ibid.
11. Petherick, p. 39.
12. *Remarks*, Postscript, p. 2.
13. Ibid., Postscript, p. 3.
14. *An Elegie on Coronel Blood* (1680).

Notes

Chapter Eighteen

1. Bodleian Library, Rawlinson MS A185, fos 473, 474.
2. *The Complete Newgate Calendar*, vol. I.
3. Bodleian Library, Rawlinson MS A185, fos 473, 474.
4. According to Burke: Montgomery-Massingberd; Marshall, *Intelligence and Espionage*, p. 205.
5. CSP, 1 Sept. 1680–31 Dec. 1681, p. 665.
6. Montgomery-Massingberd; Petherick, p. 14.
7. Burghclere, *Ormonde*, vol. II, p. 305.
8. Burghclere, *Buckingham*, p. 399
9. Hutton, pp. 443, 444.

BIBLIOGRAPHY

PRIMARY SOURCES

By the King: A proclamation. Charles R. whereas upon Tuesday, the sixth of this instant December, between the hours of six and seven in the evening, a barbarous and inhumane attempt was made upon the person and life of our right trusty and right entirely beloved cousin, and counsellor, James Duke of Ormond, etc. London: Printed by the assigns of John Bill and Christopher Barker, 1670

By the King: A proclamation for the discovery and apprehension of John Locklier, Timothy Butler, Thomas Blood, commonly called Captain Blood, John Mason, and others. London: Printed by the assigns of John Bill and Christopher Barker, Printers to the King's most Excellent Majesty, 1667

Calendar of State Papers, Domestic Series, of the Reign of Charles II, 1660–1685 (28 vols). London: H.M. Stationery Office, 1860–1939

Calendar of State Papers Relating to Ireland Preserved in the Public Record Office. London: H.M. Stationery Office, 1871–1943.

[The] Civil Survey A.D. 1654–1656. County of Meath, Vol. V., with Returns of Tithes for the Meath Baronies, R.C. Simmington (ed.). Dublin: Irish Manuscripts Commission, 1940

[An] Elegie on Coronel [sic] Blood, notorious for stealing the crown, &c. who dyed the twenty sixth of August, 1680. London: Printed by J. S., 1680

[The] Horrid Conspiracie of Such Impenitent Traytors As intended A New

Rebellion in the Kingdom of Ireland with A List of the Prisoners, and The Particular Manner of Seizing Dublin-Castle by Ludlow and his Accomplices Verbatim out of the Expresses Sent to His Majesty from the Duke of Ormonde. London: Printed for Samual Speed, 1663

[The] Journal of the House of Commons of the Kingdom of Ireland, for the 14th year of King Charles II Anno 1662 to the End of the Reign of King William the 3rd, Vol. II. Dublin

[A] Just narrative of the hellish new counter-plots of the Papists to cast the odium of their horrid treasons upon the Presbyterians . . . With an account of their particular intreigues, carried on to insnare Mr Blood, and several other considerable persons with the happy discoveries thereto. London: Printed for Dorman Newman, 1679

Life and Adventures of the Famous Colonel Blood, who seized on the person of the Duke of Ormond, and conveyed him to Tyburn, with the intention of putting him to death on a common gibbet, And Who afterwards, in the disguise of a Priest, with several of his daring Associates, obtained admittance into the Tower of London, which they robbed of the Crown, Ball, Sceptre, and other Regalia; But who was afterwards pardoned by King Charles II, who settled on him a handsome pension for life. London: Hodgson and County

[The] London Gazette, No. 528: 5–8 December, 1670; No. 572, 8–11 May, 1671

[The] Narrative of Colonel Thomas Blood, concerning the design reported to be lately laid against the life and honour of his grace George Duke of Buckingham wherein Colonel Blood is charged to have conspired with Maurice Hickey, Philip le Mar, and several others, to suborn the testimony of Samuel Ryther and Philemon Coddan to swear Buggery against the said Duke. Together with a copy of the information exhibited in the Crown Office against the said Colonel Blood, Hickey, Le Mar, and the rest. London: Printed by R. Everingham at the Seven Stars in Ave-Mary-Lane, 1680

Remarks on the Life and Death of the famed Mr. Blood, Signed: R.H. Second edition, with large additions. London: Printed for Richard Janeway, in Queens-head Alley in Pater-Noster Row, 1680

Report on the Manuscripts of the Marquis of Ormonde, K.P., Preserved at the Castle Kilkenny, Historical Manuscripts Commission

Reports of the Historical Manuscripts Commission, Reports I, III, VI, VII, VIII

SECONDARY SOURCES

Abbott, W.C., *Colonel Thomas Blood, Crown-Stealer, 1618–1680*. Reprinted, Bath: Cedric Chivers, 1970

Arnold, L.J., *The Restoration Land Settlement in County Dublin, 1660–1688*. Dublin: Irish Academic Press, 1993

Bagwell, R., *Ireland Under the Stuarts and during the Interregnum*. London: Holland Press, 1963

Barnard, T. and Fenlon, J. (eds), *The Dukes of Ormonde, 1610–1745*. Woodbridge: Boydell Press, 2000

Bayley, J., *The History and Antiquities of the Tower of London with Biographical Anecdotes of Royal and Distinguished Persons . . .*, Part I, London: Printed for T. Cadell in the Strand, 1821

Beckett, J.C., *The Making of Modern Ireland 1603–1923*. London: Faber and Faber, 1966

Blood, Bindon, *Four Score Years and Ten. Sir Bindon Blood's Reminiscences*. London: G. Bell & Sons, 1933

Brooke, P., *Ulster Presbyterianism: The Historical Perspective 1610–1970*. Dublin: Gill and Macmillan, 1987

Bryant, A., *King Charles II*. London: Longman, Green and Co., 1931

Burghclere, W., *George Villiers, 2nd Duke of Buckingham 1628–1687: A Study in the History of the Restoration*. London: John Murray, 1903

—— *The Life of James, First Duke of Ormonde, 1610–1688*. London: John Murray, 1912

Burke, J.B., *The Landed Gentry of Ireland* (4th edn). London, 1958

Carte, T., *A History of the Life of James Duke of Ormonde* (1736)

Coote, S., *Royal Survivor. A Life of Charles II*. London: Hodder & Stoughton, 1999

Davies, N., *Europe, A History*. Oxford: Oxford University Press, 1996

—— *The Isles, A History*, London: Macmillan, 1999

Dixon, W. Hepworth, *Her Majesty's Tower*, Vol. IV, 3rd edn, 1871

Fraser, A., *King Charles II*. London: Weidenfeld & Nicolson, 1992; London: Arrow Books, 1998 (page numbers in the notes refer to the Arrow Books edn)

Frost, J., *The History and Topography of the County of Clare from the Earliest Times to the Beginning of the 18th Century, with Map and Illustrations* (second edition). Dublin and Cork: Mercier Press, 1973

Greaves, R.L., *Deliver Us from Evil. The Radical Underground in Britain, 1660–1663*. New York and Oxford: Oxford University Press, 1986

—— *Enemies Under His Feet. Radicals and Nonconformists in Britain, 1664–1677*, Stanford: Stanford University Press, 1990

—— *God's Other Children. Protestant Nonconformists and the Emergence of Denominational Churches in Ireland, 1660–1700*. Stanford: Stanford University Press, 1997

Herlihy, K. (ed.), *The Politics of Irish Dissent 1650–1800*. Dublin: Four Courts Press, 1997

Hilliam, D., *Crown, Orb and Spectre, The True Stories of English Coronations*. Stroud: Sutton Publishing, 2001

Holmes, F., *The Presbyterian Church in Ireland. A Popular History*, Dublin: Columba Press, 2000

Hutton, R., *Charles the Second. King of England, Scotland, and Ireland*. Oxford: Clarendon Press, 1989

Kaye, E.W.W., *The Romance and Adventures of the Notorious Colonel Blood who Attempted to Steal the Crown Jewels from the Tower of London in the Reign of Charles II*. Manchester: John Heywood, 1903

Kilroy, P., *Protestant Dissent and Controversy in Ireland 1660–1714*. Cork: Cork University Press, 1994

MacKenzie, F., Unpublished paper on the Blood family consulted at Local Studies Library, Ennis, Co. Clare, Ireland

Marshall, A., 'Colonel Thomas Blood and the Restoration Political Scene', *The Historical Journal*, 32, 3 (1989), pp. 561–82

—— *Intelligence and Espionage in the Reign of Charles II, 1660–1685*. Cambridge: Cambridge University Press, 1994

Marvell, Andrew, *Complete Poetry*, George deForest Lord (ed.). London: Dent, 1984

Montgomery-Massingberd, H. (ed.), *Burke's Irish Family Records* (revision of 1958 edn). London: Burke's Peerage Ltd

Moody, T.W. and Martin, F.X. (eds), *The Course of Irish History*. Cork: Mercier Press, 1967

Morrill, J., *Stuart Britain: A Very Short Introduction*. Oxford: Oxford University Press, 2000

Norrington, R. (Commentary), *My Dearest Minette. The Letters between Charles II and his Sister Henrietta, Duchesse d'Orléans*. London and Chester Springs: Peter Owen, 1996

Peacock, M., *Colonel Blood, A Novel*. London: Robert Hale, 1946

Petherick, M., *Restoration Rogues*. London: Hollis and Carter, 1951

Picard, L. *Restoration London*. London: Weidenfeld & Nicolson, 1997; London: Phoenix Press, 2001 (page numbers in the notes refer to the Phoenix Press edn)

Reilly, T., *Cromwell: An Honourable Enemy*. Ireland: Brandon, 1999

Rylands, J.P., *Notes on the Families of Holcroft, of Holcroft, Co. Lancaster; Holcroft, of Vale Royal, Co. Chester; Holcroft, of Hurst, Co. Lancaster . . . Etc., with an account of their arms . . . Reprinted from the Leigh Chronicle, etc.* Lancashire, 1877

Seaward, P., *The Restoration*. London: Macmillan Education, 1991

Sobel, Dava, *Longitude*. London: Fourth Estate, 1996

Stainer, C.L., *Colonel Blood, A Play in Five Acts*. Oxford: Basil Blackwell, 1933

Weir, H.W.L., *Houses of Clare*. Clare: Ballinakella Press, 1999

Woolrych, A., *England without a King*. London: Methuen 1983

Younghusband, G., *The Jewel House*. London: Herbert Jenkins, 1921

INDEX

Index